I0767399

Seven Spheres Rising

Seven Spheres Rising

Building Micro-Cultures in Babylon

DR. ROB COVELL

Seven Spheres Rising:
Building Micro-Culture in Babylon
Dr. Rob Covell

© Printed 2024

ISBN 9798884885295

Quest Theological Institute Publishing

Cover design and inside layout
Carolyn Covell

Printed in the USA

Acknowledgements ____

I first want to thank my beautiful wife and covenant partner, Carolyn Covell: You help me accomplish the goal of writing many books and you provide the peace that empowers me to be a successful man. I am grateful for your love and your faithful prayers that strengthen me. I am a blessed man to have you forever by my side.

I also want to acknowledge my father and mother, Craig & Noelle Covell who imprinted on me the perseverance and unyielding commitment to stand in trials, fight for my destiny, and through God's grace, succeed in this wonderful life.

To my colleagues at Wagner University and HIM: You are wonderful people who are dedicated to fulfilling God's call in your lives and stewarding Dr. C. Peter Wagner's legacy. I am grateful for your partnership and work in the gospel of Jesus Christ, equipping world changers and advancing the Kingdom of God through Christian education.

Thank you, Apostle Tony Kim, for your friendship, leadership, and spiritual mentoring in my life. You are a world class leader who is an expert on cultural renewal and revitalization. I have learned so much from your leadership at HIM. I look forward to what the Lord might do through our partnership at Wagner University.

To my colleagues and family of faith at The Refuge Community Church and The Refuge School of Arts & Innovation: I appreciate you all. It is an honor to be associated with you.

A special thank you to my sailor friends Richard Maure, Chris Alvarado and Matt O'Connell: Thank you for teaching me the most wonderful experience of harnessing the wind and feeling the freedom of the ocean. SIBYC!

Lastly, a very special thanks to Apostle Che Ahn: You are a leader who operates with the upmost integrity in the fullness of faith and wisdom. It is an honor to sit at your table and learn how to lead large organizations. You have imparted to me the secret of leadership which is always prioritizing prayer, Scripture reading, and obedience to Jesus. Thank you, Papa Che!

Contents

Introduction

Seven Spheres Rising: Building Micro-Culture in Babylon is an on-ramp that is intended to light fires in the hearts of Christians. Its purpose is to give the Church of Jesus Christ a clear path into understanding the spiritual warfare that is being waged for cultural preeminence in the Global North. Many Christians instinctively are aware that Western Civilization is in decline. Christianity has lost its voice. It has lost its ability to influence and guide culture through the Biblical wisdom the Church possesses. We may be painfully aware of these things and concerned about them, but most Christian leaders and cultural stakeholders lack a Biblical worldview or congruent strategy for healing what is broken in our society. There are two reactions to this realization of the societal decline in the West: One is to raise our voices and point out everything that is wrong and protest our loss of influence; the other is to accept the loss and allow the culture to drift away from God, confirming it by promoting pessimistic eschatological doctrines that inspire the expectation of the world is getting darker because we are now in the "End Times."

Both of these reactions to the cultural drift away from God in the Global North from the Judeo-Christian, or Theistic, worldview that guided the West in previous centuries are not expedient for healing a broken culture. What is expedient to healing a broken culture that has lost its Christian inheritance is to go back to the Apostolic Gospel that produced the great prosperity, scientific advancement, architecture, art, and medical sciences that has made the West a great place to live on planet Earth. Certainly, Western Civilization has never been a utopia. There are many examples of sin in the collective history of Western political leaders and cultural influencers who brought about great suffering, oppression, wars, and death to millions of people. And glossing over the sins of Western civilization is not expedient for healing a culture either. However, the West has always been able to reform itself and become more just, more equitable, and more altruistic because concerned Christian leaders and influencers have exerted their faith, prayers, and political action through the lens of Scripture and the power of the Holy Spirit breathing on them to effect societal healing. There are many examples like William Wilberforce, Harriet Tubman, Frederick Douglas, John Wesley, and Dr. Martin Luther King Jr. who were anointed to bring systemic reformation to the West. Their lives highlight the truth that God works through people, as He guides them into their collective destinies in Him.

Isaiah 5:20-21 says:

"Woe to those who call evil good, and good evil; Who substitute darkness for light and light for darkness; Who substitute bitter for sweet and sweet for bitter Woe to those who are wise in

their own eyes and clever in their own sight!"

Isaiah's prophetic vision not only spoke to his culture that departed from the knowledge of God, but is an accurate description of the current state of affairs in the Global North. Notice the Text begins with a declaration of "woe", a Hebrew euphemism that describes prolonged dissatisfaction and pain. The Scriptures are very clear: A culture that departs from the knowledge of God will never prosper. To depart from God's order is to depart from light and embrace the closing of the mind to the wisdom of God. A people group who rejects God darkens itself unto its demise.

Currently, the Global North has its guiding ideologies that are the exact polar opposites of the type of cultural ethos that the Scriptures promote. The contrast between Deuteronomy 28 and the common cultural ethos of the modern West draws a comparative picture that is shocking to the reader. The main thrust of this work is not to highlight the obvious cultural degradation of the Global North, but to provide the holy prescription for healing society and building a better future where God can begin to partner with the Global North to bring about the type of culture and society that He can actively bless. This work is aimed at outlining the way forward for Christians who are called to foment the type of revival and reformation that produces "sheep nations" in the West.

Seven Spheres Rising: Building Micro-Culture in Babylon

In the Global North, we should never discount that the current cultural degradation is the direct result of spiritual warfare. The Western rational mind possesses a blind spot that makes it ineffective for bringing societal reformation because our common worldview is dualistic. The dualistic worldview separates sacred from secular and discounts the possibility that malevolent spiritual entities (Satan and demons) are actively opposing and attacking goodness in society through leaders and societal spheres of influence.

Seven Spheres Rising promotes a Biblical worldview that will heal the dualism in our minds and give us new lenses by which we can diagnose societal sickness without demonizing people who are made in God's image. Ephesians 6:12 frames the battle lines that we see manifesting in the Global North in a way that helps us truly understand the struggle for cultural preeminence:

> *"For our struggle is not against flesh and blood, but against the rulers, against the powers, against the world forces of this darkness, against the spiritual forces of wickedness in the heavenly places."*

Having the correct cosmology of the world God created is paramount for Christians who are interested in societal influence and reformation.

Seven Spheres Rising will key in on the necessary social structures and collective ethos that builds a City on a Hill. These are model Christian communities that create alternative institutions on a micro-level that create not only the template for reformation, but eventually become the prevailing ethos of the Global North. We need to keep in mind that we are not resurrecting an old order but instituting an order that is birthed from the revelation of the Holy Spirit in the hearts and minds of Christians. Certainly, the US Constitution is the highest Law of the land in the American context. Contemporary Christian Reformers would never desire to replace the founding documents however, we should realize that the US Constitution empowers Christian wisdom because the Judeo-Christian worldview is enshrined in the text. Because of this, modern Christian Reformers have the permission to partner with the illumination that God gives. They, too, have the wisdom to propose creative solutions for the answers that heal society and culture in order to bring the West back to God-consciousness.

This work is not exhaustive in its blueprint for cultural reformation, but it builds the foundation for other leaders, stakeholders, and influencers to begin to be inspired to build as the Spirit leads. Humanity is now at the precipice of either reformation toward Christianity and Kingdom culture, or the downward spiral described in Romans 1:18-30. We must be prepared to build with an inter-generational vision, or we lose the Global North to secular humanism and the social mental illnesses that godlessness brings. Commitment to the long strategy of culture shift requires the type of covenant thinking that has been lost in Western Christianity. Culture change is as much of a theological pursuit as it is an action. What we think about God and the future of the Church influences our daily decisions and guides the trajectory of our lives. The modern Evangelical Institution desperately needs a reformation in its systematic theology to bring the Western Church back to the Apostolic doctrines that empowered the Church in its Apostolic genesis to bring about the type of covenant commitment for cultural change to be effective.

Now, let's journey through *Seven Spheres Rising: Building Micro-Culture in Babylon* and begin to build a paradigm for the New Apostolic Reformation mindset that will change the world.

Chapter 1

God's Design in Creation

The primary mover in the collective decisions of a people group are embodied in a shared worldview. Their shared worldview is the foundation that moves the culture and influences almost everything about their lives, both personally and collectively. The cultural norms that guide society are the sum total of our agreed upon worldview as a people group. Culture is always downstream from our predominant worldview. Currently, in the Global North there are two competing worldviews with one of those worldviews taking pre-eminence in the common culture that is now moving firmly into the social morass we see today. These two competing worldviews are the Biblical/Theistic Worldview and the Humanist/Atheistic Worldview. Christians are losing the culture war because we have failed to see the importance of worldview. The institutions that build and carry Western culture are now predomi-nantly guided by the atheistic worldview. This world-view has produced alarming results that should cause concern in the hearts and minds of every Christian.

Seven Spheres Rising: Building Micro-Culture in Babylon

Christian families are surprised when their children depart from the faith and live in ways contrary to the faith of their fathers and mothers. However, we should not be surprised because culture is always the product of those who educate the children. Several generations of Western children educated by atheists have produced the exact mirror image of their worldview in our modern culture. Christian children who spend a few hours a week in church on Sunday and then spend over forty hours immersed in the atheism of the public school with its entertainment and contemporary internet content will produce the fruit of the table from where they have dined. The atheism that drives institutional influence in the West is so cemented in secular humanism that it is irredeemable on a macro-level. There are certainly pockets of rural America that may be redeemable through Christian influence, but the policy making power structures in high places are too far gone. The best example is our failing public school systems and universities that are thoroughly indoctrinating our future leaders and influencers by inculcating them into an antichrist inspired mind that hates God and rejects the classic Western Christian ethos.

Let's explore and contrast these two competing worldviews so that we may understand how worldview builds the foundation that creates systemic change in cultures, either good or bad.

The Theistic Worldview ___________________

People who have a supernatural belief in how the world was created have a theistic worldview. This includes all religions. Because this work is a piece of Christian scholarship, we will only be concerned with what the Bible reveals about the subject of cosmology. However, it is important to realize that atheism is a modern anomaly creation myth, and that at no time in history have people groups ever embraced the atheistic construct of reality and the universe until the modern era. The Biblical worldview finds its origin in the revelation of God in the very first verse of Genesis Chapter One. Genesis 1:1 begins with, *"In the beginning, God created the heavens and the earth."* The Bible is unapologetic in its position that the Godhead pre-existed creation. It is transcendent from the construct of time, always existing and is complete within Itself. The Godhead is uncreated, omniscient, omnipotent, and omnipresent. The first revelation of God in the creation narrative is that He is a Father. It is important to recognize this because God is relational in Himself: Father, Son, and Holy Spirit. He is also relational towards His creation, especially to people made in His image and likeness.

As the Genesis narrative unfolds, we see increasingly intimate interactions between God and His creation. The LORD God creates complex systems that are a product of His intelligent design to curate a world

in which mankind can dwell with Him, living in relationship with a loving, wholly benevolent Father God. On
the sixth day, God crowns His cosmos with a creation
like Himself to reflect His nature and character to the
rest of creation. Genesis 1:26-28 says:

> *"Then God said, "Let us make man [the
> generic term for people] in our image, after our
> likeness. And let them have dominion over the
> fish of the sea and over the birds of the heavens
> and over the livestock and over all the earth
> and over every creeping thing that creeps on
> the earth." So God created man in his own
> image, in the image of God he created him;
> male and female he created them. And God
> blessed them. And God said to them, "Be fruit-
> ful and multiply and fill the earth and subdue it,
> and have dominion over the fish of the sea and
> over the birds of the heavens and over every
> living thing that moves on the earth."*

In the revelation of the creation of humanity, we
see something unique and valuable that was born in
the Father heart of God. It is by the grace of God that
people would be endowed with a dominion over God's
creation in ways that mimic God's superior dominion
over all things. People have been given the creativity,
wisdom, ability, and power to manage God's created
order consisting of all things on the earth. The next
thing we see in the Text is that created humanity reflects

the Creator in their ability to produce and multiply generations of many made in Imago Dei. Humanity was given the charge to heavenize earth and expand their dominion to its fullest expression within the will of God. This pre-Fall intention of God's heart was corrupted by sin in Eden however, God being omniscient, omnipotent, and omnipresent was never surprised by the Fall. Authenticity in relationship can only be proved by the ability to love through obedience. The first Adam failed in his love for God; the Second Adam (Jesus Christ) prevailed. In love, as an obedient Son who never sinned, Jesus re-empowered the dominion mandate for humanity by His death on the cross and victory over the grave.

The guiding ethos of the theistic worldview promotes the truth that God is a loving Father who created the world we see through His intelligent design. Humanity possesses unique intrinsic value because we are made in His image. The time/space continuum is being guided by a benevolent God who is restoring unto humanity that which was corrupted and lost in Eden. The theistic worldview is grounded in purpose that brings meaning to our lives and to the lives of others. It holds that the universe is founded on the intelligent design of God, and science reveals the wonderful mysteries of God's creative power and benevolence in creation. The theistic worldview holds that people reflect and mimic God's superior mind and consciousness. The theistic worlview stands on the foundation that truth is a revelation and is found only in God's Person. Humanity has been organized in ways that God has determined for us. We will explore these truths in greater detail as we develop this chapter, but for now, let's contrast the theistic worldview to the atheistic worldview.

The Atheistic Worldview

The construct of the atheistic worldview is built on the formulaic idea that matter (which has always existed) plus time (which has always existed) plus random chance has produced the cosmos that we live in. The implications of the atheistic worldview are a radical departure from the value-based creation narrative that defines the theistic worldview. In an atheistic worldview, humanity possesses no intrinsic value because humanity is a product of material, time, and random chance with instinctive biological processes. In addition to this, truth is a construct of the human mind and culture is built not on a revelation of God, but on the arbitrary ideas of the humanistic oligarchy that exerts its influence on the rest of mankind through the institutions that guide it. In the atheistic worldview, humanity is not accountable to a Creator for the individual and collective decisions of a people group. This cosmology is divorced from revealed truth and morality. It is now making its own way redefining reality and culture. The atheistic worldview has no God for its anchor or standard from which morals and ethics flow. These are not immutable, but mutable and can change in any direction. The atheistic worldview fails to answer the primary question of the human experience which is, *"What is the meaning of life?"* Atheism naturally produces nihilism and by its very nature is destructive because it empowers sin to prosper without restraint. The wages of sin is always death. Chaos cultures bring the death of the nuclear family, the death of safety in society, and the death of millions by democide. Chaos cultures bring the death of culture.

The atheistic worldview is dangerous because it empowers the influencers and authorities that guide culture to make arbitrary decisions about any subject and call it truth. This means that the concept of truth is always evolving and what is true today may not be true in the future. The atheistic worldview is devolution of reality and will never produce the freedom it promises because its cosmology is divorced from God. We will explore the implications of the atheistic worldview in greater detail as we seek to understand how to reform the current culture we live in by creating Christian micro-cultures that change the world as we progress in this work.

God's Cultural Design

The theistic worldview promotes the idea of a relational God who is involved with His creation and with people who are made in His image. The theistic way of thinking about creation recognizes both intelligent design and God's relational interactions in the creative order. The natural progression of thinking about intelligent design is the idea of natural order. God does not design things that do not work well. It only makes sense that God ordered human life to live well in some type of cultural organization. As the Genesis narrative unfolds, we see humanity begins to organize in aggregate groups and express itself in seven spheres of culture. Sociologists and archeologists have identified these seven intersecting spheres of Religion, Family, Education, Government, Economy, Arts/Entertainment, and News/Media. Reform theologians, Abraham Kuyper and Francis Shaeffer, used this "sphere" terminology and popularized it in Christian theology as corresponding to God's created order for humanity to express itself and live in peace with each other as people began to congregate. These seven spheres of culture create the social institutions that define the social contract by which people agree to live together. When people live together in significant numbers these seven spheres of cultural intersection become manifest no matter where in the world they are living. Theologians have looked at these seven spheres of cultural intersection and determined that these seven spheres exist because God designed them as the vehicle by which humanity would enjoy life and find their purpose.

When we consider the Genesis 1:26-28 dominion

mandate given to humanity, we can see that God created a social structure for fulfilling the dominion mandate. The effects of the Fall in Eden corrupted the purity of these seven spheres of culture with supernatural evil that influences humanity along with humanity's sinful and rebellious heart toward God. However, the time/space continuum as unfolded through the Biblical narrative reveals that God is entirely committed to redeeming individual people, nations, and the whole cosmos from corruption, sin and death through the revelation of Messiah. The atonement that Jesus Christ accomplished on the cross not only redeems individuals from the wages of sin and gives the promise of eternal life, but the atonement also offers the promise of cultural redemption with the climatic manifestation of a new heavens and a new earth that restores the Edenic conditions of the pre-Fall era of human history. This is the great hope and meta-narrative of Messiah.

The seven spheres of culture reveal the mandate of the Church and appeal to Her to consider the deeper work of the atonement that Jesus accomplished on the cross: the mandate to become a Kingdom people who accomplish revealing the widespread knowledge of God throughout the whole earth. We are not just speaking about evangelizing the world but fulfilling the mandate that our Lord and Savior Jesus Christ charged us with. In Matthew 28:18-20, Jesus says:

Seven Spheres Rising: Building Micro-Culture in Babylon

"All authority has been given to Me in heaven and on earth. Go therefore and make disciples of all the nations, baptizing them in the name of the Father and the Son and the Holy Spirit, teaching them to observe all that I command- ed you; and lo, I am with you always, even to the end of the age."

Jesus casts a vision for the Gospel that eclipses the salvation of only individuals but includes whole people groups that would become obedient to the leadership of Jesus Christ. Jesus never gives the Church the option to fail. He puts forth the expectation that His Church is successful throughout the millennia in Her Gospel labor. After all, She is endued with the delegated authority from Christ Himself and is empowered by the anointing of the Holy Spirit to accomplish Her purpose.

For the Church in the Global North to prosper in Her call, there needs to be a radical departure from what is not working. This requires a return to the Apostolic Gospel that is fueled by the renewed mind that has been washed by the Word and empowered by the Holy Spirit.

For far too long, the Church in the Global North has adopted the Western dualistic worldview of the secular and sacred divide. This compartmentalization of the human experience between secular and sacred, along with the negative premillennial eschatology that is so popular in the American Evangelical Institution, has cast a vision for a Church that expects the world to grow darker. It's expectation of a great falling away with a withdrawal from culture, and the expectation of increasing governmental tyranny leaves the American Evangelical Institution powerless to turn the West back to God. It is no wonder the Church in the Global North exists in a post-Christian culture and She is fine with it, all the while complaining about the condition of the world around Her.

A revival in worldview empowers the rediscovery of the truth that Jesus is Lord of all, and all things serve Christ to bring all glory, power and honor to Him. If the Church in the Global North has no vision for the glory of Jesus to be present in the seven spheres of culture, then She does not and cannot receive the faith to accomplish Her dominion mandate to heavenize earth. God's creation was intelligently designed to glorify Him in all things. The Biblical expectation is that God is to be glorified in Family, Religion, Education, Government, Economy, Arts/Entertainment, and Media. It is the Church activated as leaven in world that causes the whole loaf to rise to the point where the knowledge of God will cover the earth as the waters cover the sea.

Vocation is Calling and Ministry ___________

One of the main drivers of Christian withdrawal from

the seven spheres of culture is the Platonic dualism that lives in the minds of Western Christians. Dualism is removed when the secular vs. sacred divide is integrated into a Biblical cosmology, which is all things for Christ and all things unto Christ. Colossians 3:23-24 says:

> *"Whatever you do, do your work heartily, as for the Lord rather than for men, knowing that from the Lord you will receive the reward of the inheritance. It is the Lord Christ whom you serve."*

The seven spheres of culture cosmology extends to us the richness of co-laboring with the Lord in the context of authentic relationships with God that change the world. Each one of us has a place in God's world to bring Him glory through what we find our hands doing. Whether we are changing tires, changing diapers, leading companies, selling goods, or serving people we do all things unto the Lord. Our lives are our ministry. For far too long the evangelical ideal for people is to serve the Church in full time ministry. Anything less is not valued with the same significance as professional clergy. The elite Christians that served God in ministry were the only ones who were honored and esteemed. The rest of us were told to pay tithes, warm the pews, and buy into the "vision" of the leaders that guide the local church. However, the truth is that all work is holy unto the Lord and all work is a sacred pursuit that brings Him glory. The sphere of religion is only one intersecting circle of the human experience. Though it is an important one, it is no more important than family, education, economy, arts, media, and government because all life lives before the face of God.

The whole world is the Lord's and Jesus is Lord of all things. This means that the seven spheres of culture are not only the mission field but are also holy ministry to Christ. Ezekiel 47 casts the prophetic vision of water flowing out from the Church and giving life every-where the river flows, even making saltwater com-pletely fresh. This speaks of the power of the Spirit-filled Church's ability to bring transformation to the world. In addition to this, the trees of healing that bear fruit in all seasons nourish the people and bring redemption to the nations. Notice that the greatest transforma-tion takes place away from the Temple from which the water began to flow. Ezekiel's prophetic vision of the Church reorients our expectations of the success of the Church and declares the Church is the change agent that systemically reforms whole people groups in the world. As society is organized by God in seven spheres, the Church flows living water into those spheres and renews those spaces. Isaiah 60:11 says:

> *"Your gates will be open continually; They will not be closed day or night, So that men may bring to you the wealth of the nations, With*

their kings led in procession."

What we see in this prophetic vision of the Church is the Church waters the world with the transforming knowledge of Christ, and into the Church flows the wealth of the nations. There is both outflow of blessings and inflows of blessings. Our expectation is a constant cycle of both watering unto transformation, and the inflow of great blessings from those who have been transformed. It is a beautiful prophetic portrait of the collective Church of Jesus Christ moving in Spirit-filled glory and purpose to heavenize earth and advance the Kingdom of God until the glorious return of Jesus Christ.

The Foundation of Culture Change

The foundation of culture change is built in the long-term commitment of Christians committed to a strategy of generational reformation in the seven spheres of society. It is paramount to understand that all countercultures become mainstream when passion for change is married to vision, and then those who are committed to cultural reformation prioritize their lives towards that end. Thus, an unstoppable movement is released in the seven spheres of culture. It is important to realize that throughout history, Christianity has been the true counterculture because it stands in direct opposition to the antichrist Babylonian systems that are blinded from the light of God and rule the world. We have a historical legacy of moving from an insignificant counterculture into becoming the pre-dominant culture throughout the New Testament era. This is because the Church of Jesus Christ has the spiritual authority, mandate, and blessing from God to reform the nations we exist in. May we rediscover this truth in the Global North!

This type of thinking will require Christians to not only develop a true theistic worldview, but to also cultivate the long-term passion, vision, and generational priorities it takes to sustain a movement of culture change in the West. The necessity of building break-away institutions is the first work we should be engaging in if we will be successful in our cultural reformation efforts. Many have proposed that Christians infiltrate existing institutions of power in the Global North. This may have been a viable option in decades past however, in the current American context, institutional ethics are much too saturated with atheistic infiltration and have become too far gone for a successful reverse.

It is time to admit that we forfeited institutional power to the Babylonian spirit and have lost our cultural influence. It is now time to start at the same place the early Church found itself in at the beginning of the First Century Roman Empire. As in past centuries, Christians will need to create self-existing micro-cultures that stand as alternatives to the dominant cultural institutions of power. This means we will need to move in proximity to one another. We will need to work hard to heal families and maintain healthy marriages. We will need to build schools, found new liberal arts universities, run for local political office, and create our own micro-economies that will transfer the wealth of the pagans to the people of God. We must regroup and create Christian communities that will build the momentum to change the world. The good news is that God has already given us the grace to accomplish Matthew 28:18-20.

In the following chapter, we will take the next essential step in building the foundation for a seven sphere cultural change. This next step is learning the type of critical thinking that is necessary for evaluating what is important, valuable, and truthful so we can determine the best decisions for our own personal lives, and for society as a whole. A theistic worldview joined to a critical thinking process is the tip of the spear that guides a reformer's vision for culture change.

Chapter 2

What is Truth?______

There are three essential points of contact that are necessary for determining what truth is. The current expression of public education is designed to cultivate the masses into easily controlled people who can be harvested, resourced, and socially engineered by those who are building toward an atheistic society, free from the accountability of God-consciousness in the people. Our current educational learning institutions do not teach people how to think critically, but rather they teach people compliance through social pressure. The art of dialogue, rhetoric, debate, and the exchange of ideas in the public space are not prioritized in public education. Therefore, we have produced several generations of ideologically engineered drones enslaved to a humanistic hivemind. The fruit of public education is conformity and compliance rooted in atheistic humanism. That is why we see the complete redefinition of morality, ethics, and the socially acceptable norms in the common culture led by those who control the current institutions of power.

Critical thinking flows from three points of contact: **ontology**, **axiology**, and **epistemology**. The theistic worldview stands on the foundation that all truth is a revelation from God. God Himself is truth and God has revealed truth to people in multi-dimensional ways from creation itself to His Word. The three points of contact for discovering truth – ontology, axiology, and epistemology – are the framework by which we test cultural ideas and theories. Now, let's define these words and make them accessible so we can apply them to the world around us and discover how to determine what is true, pure, and good.

Ontology

Ontology simply means the study of being. In the Christian context, God is the One true Being, who is self-existent, omnipotent, omnipresent, and omniscient. Our being (existence) is the fruit of His Being because we are made in His image and likeness. Therefore, our first point of contact when dealing with any subject we are seeking truth about is to consider what God says, feels, and thinks about that subject. We learn the emotions of God's heart, discovering His nature and character in the Scriptures. Additionally, we can also receive revelation, illumination, and confirmation about anything as we pray, listen, and respond to God's voice. Because God is wholly relational in His interactions with His sons and daughters, we can be assured that God has something to say to us about every issue of life. We only need to discover what He says in the Word of God, in prayer, and through any other means of relational interaction with Him.

When we are faced with processing the current culture in which we live, we should begin with looking at all points of contact in the context of the Person of God, which is our ontological first step. Many things in our common culture are contrary to things that God has already decided in His Word. It is important to note that God's Law, standards, decisions, and judgments are perfect because He is perfect. We should never change or adapt our positions to agree with the common culture, but we should disciple the common culture toward the things that God has already said in His Word. The reason the collective Church of Jesus Christ is not leading the culture towards God is because we have not engaged our culture through the ontological lens of what God thinks, feels, has said, and wants to do about a thing. Because we have not considered this very fundamental starting point in the critical thinking process, many in the Church are confused about LGBTQ+ issues, progressive political issues, socialism, communism, education, abortion, divorce, justice, and entertainment. However, when we consider God's Being at the center of life, then we have the starting point by which all things should conform.

The second step in the ontological process is how does the issue we are exploring affect our being?

Seven Spheres Rising: Building Micro-Culture in Babylon

Once we know what God has said, now we can process how the particular issue affects our being. Our being should be inculcated into His Being. After all, Jesus said in John 17:11, *"that they be one, even as We are one."* Our lives are the true sum total of the choices we have made. What we decide in the everyday sets the directional compass of our lives. On an aggregate level, our societal trajectories are determined by the collective choices of a people who either agree or disagree with God. This second step considers our being, or in other words, our identity as a covenant people in relationship to the LORD.

When we process through the lens of how a particular issue or subject affects God's Being and then think through how the issue or subject affects our being, and finally, how the issue or subject affects others' being, we are now equipped to begin the process of determining what is true. That last step of considering how an issue or subject affects another's being is important because considering others will test our hearts and reveal our emotional health. It will reveal areas in our lives that need emotional healing. The three-fold ontological process is the primary starting point for beginning to understand the issues of life, culture, and societal direction. Currently, the common culture is being socially engineered to begin to process current events or issues with the starting point of the human heart, not ever considering God's Person, His nature and character, or His Word. In Jeremiah 17:9, it is written:

> *"The heart is more deceitful than all else and is desperately sick; Who can understand it?"*

To deny God by using the human heart's perception of social issues as a starting point is not the pathway to wisdom. One only needs to look at the current state of affairs to see that there is no wisdom, no goodness, and no Godly illumination in this modern-day Babylon we are living in.

Discovering truth begins with the ontological process and then moves the subject forward to the next movement of discerning what truth is, which is axiology. In the next section, we will explore this second point of contact.

Axiology

The definition of axiology is the study of value, or goodness. The axiological method begins with discerning the value or goodness that God places on a subject, issue, or thing. The axiological starting point is always the revelation and illumination that He gives us in His Word, the Holy Scriptures. God's Word reveals all wisdom, value, goodness, truth, and love to our lived reality.

Seven Spheres Rising: Building Micro-Culture in Babylon

The primary place to start examining a subject or issue through the lens of axiology is to consider the value, goodness, or importance of that subject or issue in light of what God says about it. Whatever value God places on a subject or issue should be the same value we apply. This is very important, especially in terms of navigating the atheistic humanism that is currently guiding the Western ethos. For example, the LGBTQ+ lobby is driving national and global policies even though this lobby is a very small fraction of the population. This lobby will always be a permanent subculture in any people group because God's intelligent design for the continued propagation of generations is the traditional nuclear family, and not homosexual relationships. In the context of ontology and axiology, this lobby is not the norm and therefore should not have the power to determine the direction of cultures or nations. Individual civil rights in liberal republican democracies provide enough societal protection for all non-conformists. This is the value that recognizes Imago Dei (the image of God) in all people. It is one thing to recognize Imago Dei in all people thus guaranteeing their individual civil rights to live as they please; it is another thing to give an atheistic subculture the keys to undo the normative social design for culture that is established by God.

Axiology gives us the grid by which all issues and subjects are assigned value and are placed in their determinate positions in God's sphere-based order.

Some issues possess higher intrinsic value or influence than others, and axiology is the scale by which we evaluate their value and goodness. To think axiologically means that when we approach a subject, we consider the value and goodness that God places on that subject or issue. We then assign its place on the axiological scale. Again, God's Word is the always the guiding illumination that reveals being, value, and goodness to everything concerning humanity. To deny God's Word as the guide to all matters of the heart and life, is to deny ourselves the blessed life of peace with God, peace within ourselves, and peace with the people around us.

Epistemology the next and final point of contact in the process of determining what truth is.

Epistemology

The definition of epistemology is the investigatory process of discovering and distinguishing between belief and opinion. Every person has opinions and feelings, however, not all of those opinions and feelings are grounded in objective truth. I am sure we can all point to a time in our lives when we felt strongly about something and then later changed our minds because we learned more information that revealed truth to us about that matter. The concept of truth is absolute. Truth cannot be hidden, contained, or distorted for very long because truth always comes to light. In Psalm 119:160, it reads:

> *"The sum of Your word is truth, and every one of Your righteous ordinances is ever-lasting."*

This verse places the things that God has said in His Word as preeminent above all other things. The Scriptures reveal truth because God is truth. He is the inventor of truth in the human experience, all things will be judged by God in light of His truth. There are many other verses which illustrate this point but, for the sake of brevity, we will move our exploration of determining what truth is forward.

Truth cannot be subjective because subjectivity is not grounded in objective facts and provable metrics of determination. The Bible teaches us that God determines truth. God has defined truth, and His truth is eternal because He is eternally existing. Epistemology is the process by which we verify opinion and feelings. Because of this, we need to have a standard by which opinion and feelings conform. This standard is the perfect standard that God sets in His Word. We can see that the acceptance of something being true is always decided by the Scriptures. This is not to deny nuance, as many Bible interpretations have been interpreted with the lack of the disciplined hermeneutics by which we should systematically study God's Word. Nevertheless, there are many things that are plain to comprehend and much of the Bible can be easily understood, especially the things that God says about everyday life like morality, ethics, and justice.

The process by which we determine truth begins with feelings, opinions, and experiences because from these things flow the issues of life. We can now take our feelings, opinions, and experiences and process them first through an ontological consideration (being), then through the axiological consideration (value/goodness), and finally through the epistemological consideration which is discerning and distinguishing truth from our opinion, feelings, or lived experiences. In the pursuit of truth, God's Word is at the center. It is the absolute standard by which each of these considerations is processed. This is the foundation for rational, objective, and logical interpretation of any subject. The most concerning thing about the times in which we live is the departure from the awareness of God and His Word in the seven spheres of culture. When a culture departs from a theistic worldview, then that culture has no anchor in objective reality and all things become subjective and arbitrary. The corresponding fruit is cultural anarchy and the chaos that we now see beginning to manifest. The hive-mind of the people becomes mentally ill when God is not at the center of that culture. The current "gender theory" teaching where gender is a construct of the mind and feelings, and not determined by biological design, is evidence the culture has departed from the ontological, axiological, and epistemological process of determining truth from the fountain of God's Word.

It is important we begin to teach our children this three-fold process of ontology, axiology, and epistemology to determine what truth is by using God's Word as the guiding light of illumination and wisdom. People who are empowered to think are people who are empowered to bring good solutions to society and culture. This is the type of people who cannot be controlled by collectivism, tyrannical political leaders,or the collective mental illness of the progressive intolerance that we see emerging in the West. The most powerful thing that will stop the current destructive path we are on in the West is a people empowered to think logically using the three-fold template outlined in this chapter.

As this book unfolds, each chapter will highlight the strategies for transformative leadership that will build cultures that God would bless. In the next chapter, we will look at the theology that gives the Church of Jesus Christ the mandate to engage and be successful in a seven sphere culture shift.

Chapter 3

The Kingdom is Now

L et's discover the theology that empowered the Apostolic Church during the first few centuries of its existence. When we explore the ancient Church, we see a stark contrast between its success and the success of the modern Church in the Global North. The ancient Church was not without its difficulties and challenges. For example, the early Church endured the persecutions of non-believing Jews and pagan Romans from the dangerous heresies of the gnostics, Nestorians, Arians, and other false teachings that emerged in the immediate Apostolic/Post-Apostolic ages. However, in the midst of these challenges, the ancient Church prospered through radical signs and wonders that fueled its success as it preached the Gospel of the Kingdom. Justin Martyr, in his writings, mentioned signs, wonders, and spiritual gifts being present in the Church and were in operation during his lifetime. Here are two quotes from Justin Martyr found in his book, *Dialogue with Trypho* (155-160AD):

> *"Daily some [of you] are becoming disciples in the name of Christ, and quitting the path of error; who are also receiving gifts, each as he is worthy, illumined through the name of this Christ. For one receives the spirit of understanding, another of counsel, another of strength, another of healing, another of fore-knowledge, another of teaching, and another of the fear of God."*

> *"For the prophetical gifts remain with us, even to the present time. And hence you ought to understand that [the gifts] formerly among your nation have been transferred to us."*

Besides these two quotes, there is a vast amount of evidence from the writings of the early Church Fathers who wrote about the continuance of the sign gifts of the Spirit in the Post-Apostolic era. Many more quotes exist confirming the continuance of the gifts of the Holy Spirit, miracles, healings, and even some resurrections from the dead that are mentioned by the early Church, yet for the sake of time we will move on. Now, let's explore a short survey of Scriptures that unveil the Gospel of the Kingdom to us.

The Gospel of the Kingdom _______________

The first Scripture we will explore in this section is Matthew 4:23:

"Jesus was going throughout all Galilee, teaching in their synagogues and proclaiming the gospel of the kingdom, and healing every kind of disease and every kind of sickness among the people."

Most Western Christians in the Global North equate the Gospel of Jesus Christ with a message about God's gracious love for humanity demonstrated in the Man Jesus Christ, whom the Father sent to die for the sins of humanity by His death on a cross, His resurrection from grave confirming His sacrifice, and His ascension. The Good News is that, by faith, all who believe would receive the free gift of eternal life. The core of the statements above are true and powerful. They contain the basic truth of salvation through faith in Jesus Christ to those who believe and confess them. As amazing and powerful as these statements are, they are not the Apostolic Gospel of the New Testament Church, nor do these statements mirror the words and ministry of Jesus Christ. The tradition in the Global North of minimizing the power and authority of Jesus Christ has resulted in a Gospel message that is devoid of the spiritual power that confirms the words of the Gospel. 2 Timothy 3:5 says:

"...holding to a form of godliness, although they have denied its power; Avoid such men as these."

This verse could be a fitting indictment of a Western Church that has embraced the words of Christ but possesses an expression of Christianity that lacks the power to transform the people or reform the societies that they live in. This is an important point to realize because an intellectual approach to the Gospel will always produce minimal results. The best example of the failure of the intellectual Gospel was Paul's attempt in Acts 17:22-34 to use rationalization to preach Christ at the Areopagus in Athens. Every other example in Acts shows Paul marrying spiritual power to the message of Messiah, and then fathering the move of the Holy Spirit to plant churches, equip leaders, and expand the Church regionally throughout the seven spheres of culture.

Paul's next stop after his failure in Athens was Corinth, where he experienced a great move of God, a vision from Christ, and six months of fruitful ministry that produced a city-wide revival. It is interesting in his first letter to the Corinthians that he only approached them with the message of Christ and a demonstration of spiritual power. Paul writes in 1 Corinthians 2:3-4:

> *"...and my message and my preaching were not in persuasive words of wisdom, but in demonstration of the Spirit and of power, so that your faith would not rest on the wisdom of men, but on the power of God."*

Notice that in Athens Paul used "words of wisdom" and in Corinth, Paul employed the simple message of Christ married to the power of the Holy Spirit to authenticate his message. This is the clearest example of what the Gospel of the Kingdom looks like in living color.

If we look at Jesus' ministry in Galilee and Judea, we see the pattern of preaching, teaching, and a demonstration of the power of the Holy Spirit whenever Jesus ministered to the people. In every Gospel account, Jesus' pattern was to release both words of life and spiritual power to authenticate that His authoritative rule and reign was present and about to be inaugurated on the earth. Matthew 9:35 reads:

> *"Jesus was going through all the cities and villages, teaching in their synagogues and proclaiming the gospel of the kingdom, and healing every kind of disease and every kind of sickness."*

Here, again, we see that the Gospel of the Kingdom template is teaching, proclamation, and demonstrations of spiritual power that confirm the message of Messiah. The book of Acts follows the same template of presenting the Gospel of Jesus Christ with words of life and demonstrations of power that authenticate the message. Both the Gospels and Acts mention the "Gospel of the Kingdom" or the "Kingdom of God" terminology in the context of proclaiming the message that Messiah has come. In the West, we have built an expression of Gospel proclamation that is divorced from its inherent confirming spiritual power. One of the reasons we have built this expression of the Gospel of Jesus Christ in the West is because our collective experience in Gospel proclamation is rooted in the intellectual Western mind and not the Biblical template for advancing the Kingdom of God, as outlined in Scripture.

A New King is Proclaimed

In this next section, we will look at three more Scriptures that will help us see the hopeful expectation for the success of the Church through its proclamation of the Gospel of the Kingdom. The great success of the Apostolic Era Church was truly remarkable. In fact, the Global Church still stands on the foundation that was built in the First Century as documented in the book of Acts and in the Apostolic Letters of the New Testament. The expectation Jesus has for His Church is that the Bride (His Church) will prosper in the endeavor to spread the knowledge of Himself among every people group in His creation.

The first Scripture we will examine that outlines the template of presenting the Gospel through the pattern of words of life and works of power that authenticate our message of Messiah is Mark

16:15-17. It reads:

> *"And He said to them, "Go into all the world and preach the gospel to all creation. He who has believed and has been baptized shall be saved; but he who has disbelieved shall be condemned. These signs will accompany those who have believed: in My name they will cast out demons, they will speak with new tongues;"*

In these verses, Jesus gives a very clear directive to God's people concerning the pattern of Gospel proclamation.

First, Jesus commands us to go. This means that wherever we are, kingdom opportunities surround us. In every place we find ourselves, being a witness for Christ is commanded. Notice that Jesus does not contextualize our going, but simply commands us to go and represent Him. Though we need to move in wisdom and illumination concerning where we are to go, we should not over spiritualize our going, but rather embrace the simple truth that wherever we are, there He is also. Far too many of us have divided our "secular" lives from our "spiritual" lives therefore deceiving ourselves into believing the lie that Jesus rules our spiritual lives but not the whole world we live in. The truth is that Jesus Christ is Lord of all things, not just simply the Lord of our Sundays.

Second, Jesus describes what our going would look like. Works of spiritual power would accompany our message and confirm that Jesus is the resurrected Lord over all creation and every situation. These works that confirm the Gospel of Kingdom are authority over demons, spiritual gifts of the Holy Spirit in operation, and healing. Mark 16:18 concludes Jesus' directive with spiritual symbolism that describes the spiritual authority of the Church over evil and sin, and concludes with, *"They will lay hands on the sick, and they will recover."* The Greek word for recover in the text is **kalōs**. The definition of this word is interesting because it is used in a wide range of ways that describe a state of goodness. The word means, "beautifully, excellent and well." This is important to note because Jesus heals the whole person. Most importantly, we need healing from our sin that separates us from the Father. After this, we need to continue to be healed in various ways from emotional healing and physical healing, all the way to societal healing. When Jesus is Lord over all things in a culture, then beauty, excellence, and wellness follow in the wake of His leadership.

The next Scripture we will explore reveals our hopeful expectation for a new King Who has been crowned over all creation. It is found in Matthew 24:14. Although the direct context of this verse refers to the success of the Church in the Apostolic Era just before the destruction of Jerusalem in AD70, it does not do violence to text to suggest that the expectation of the continued success Gospel of the Kingdom continues throughout the whole of Church history. Matthew 24:14 reads:

> *"This gospel of the kingdom shall be preached in the whole world as a testimony to all the nations, and then the end will come."*

Certainly, the Apostolic Church had spread the Gospel of Jesus Christ through the whole civilized Roman world. In the context of the times and culture when the Gospel of Mark was written, the reference to the "whole world" is a direct reference to the Roman Empire and the people groups contained therein. Paul writes in Romans 1:8:

> *"First, I thank my God through Jesus Christ for you all, because your faith is being proclaimed throughout the whole world."*

The Apostle Paul uses the same language and is referring to the Roman Empire in Romans 1:8. However, the expectation remains that the Bride of Christ – the Church – is successful in her proclamation of the Gospel into every people group in His creation. For as long as people continue to be born, there is a Gospel to proclaim from generation to generation, from century to century, and millennium to millennium. Matthew 24:14 teaches us that the Gospel of the Kingdom is a testimony to all nations (ethnos - people groups) and will remain so until the glorious coming of our Lord Jesus at the end of this Kingdom Age.

The last Scripture we will look at that reveals the rule and reign of Jesus Christ through His Church is Matthew 28:18-19. Matthew 28:18-19 reads:

> *"And Jesus came up and spoke to them, saying, "All authority has been given to Me in heaven and on earth. Go therefore and make disciples of all the nations, baptizing them in the name of the Father and the Son and the Holy Spirit, teaching them to observe all that I commanded you; and lo, I am with you always, even to the end of the age."*

In these verses, Jesus explicitly says that He possesses all authority over creation. That is a tremendous concept to grasp because Jesus clearly stands in the place of dominion and power over all things in creation. Western Christians tend to believe that Jesus will be King when He returns. This type of thinking robs Jesus of His rightful place as the King that possesses all dominion, power, and authority over all creation currently. The modern Evangelical Institution of the West has embraced a lesser narrative by promoting the idea that the Kingdom of God will be coming in the future and is not presently present in the Person of Jesus Christ living in His people. This lesser narrative does not empower the modern Western Evangelical Church to live its Scriptural identity in Matthew 28:18-19 to accomplish the Great Commission in its fullness.

The command to go in the same authority that Jesus possesses is implied in the Text. Because Christ is the risen Lord and He lives in us, we are authorized to use His delegated authority to redeem the world and accomplish His vision for it. Notice in the Text that the Church makes disciples of all people groups. This is amazing because the expectation Jesus has for His Church is that She would evangelize the nations and that the whole aggregate of people would become His disciples. This does not mean that all will be Christians, but that a significant amount of people will have become Christians so as to become the guiding light that illuminates the nation and guides its course. The Gospel in the West has been individualized to the extent that we tend to approach our evangelization efforts in one off opportunities to become a follower of Christ. The Scriptures present the pattern that the Gospel is a people movement where whole aggregates of people move into Christ simultaneously. We see this Biblical pattern of people group evangelism in Acts where whole families, cities, and regions receive the Gospel and crown Christ as their collective King.

Lastly, in Matthew 28:18-19 we see Jesus will be presently present in our Gospel preaching work. He says He is with us "even to the end of the age." This means that Jesus is actively partnering with His Church to fulfill the vision of an "evangelized world" that has become obedient to the rule and reign of Christ through the agency of the Church. If Christ is with us, how can we ever expect to fail in accomplishing His desires? The Gospel of the Kingdom is life, healing, and leadership to the world as the Church is faithful to the call in Matthew 28:18-19. The Western Church desperately needs an upgrade in its expectation and proclamation of the Gospel. A Gospel that is missing its spiritual power and its vision for world dominion will never be effective in the Great Commission or its mandate to redeem the world for Christ.

Jesus is Ruling and Reigning Now ________

The theological illumination that empowers societal and cultural reformation is understanding that Jesus Christ is currently ruling and reigning as its rightful ruler. Ephesians 1:20-23 says:

> *"...that he worked in Christ when he raised him from the dead and seated him at his right hand in the heavenly places, far above all rule and authority and power and dominion, and above every name that is named, not only in this age but also in the one to come. And he put all things under his feet and gave him as head over all things to the church, which is his body,*

the fullness of him who fills all in all."

This verse is emphatic about Jesus currently ruling and reigning over His creation. His Church is an avenue through which His kingdom authority is expressed in the world. Jesus is the Sovereign of the cosmos and nothing in His world is divorced from His Lordship. This does not mean that Jesus endorses the evil and corruption in the world currently, but that all things are accountable to Him. In time, everything is reconciled in Christ either through His graceful mercy or through His judgment.

Revelation 4:11 also emphasizes the current dominion of Jesus Christ. It reads:

"Worthy are you, our Lord and God, to receive glory and honor and power, for you created all things, and by your will they existed and were created."

It is clear in the Text that the Godhead possesses all dominion and authority in the past, present, and future. Western Christians should ask themselves, *"How is Jesus actually ruling and reigning currently?"* At the time this book in your hands was written, it appears that the geopolitical landscape of the world is firmly under the control of the evil one. We must remind ourselves that perception and opinion do not always align with the truth. Additionally, premillennial eschatology proponents have remained the major voice in modern evangelical Christians, though that narrative is changing slowly back to a more traditional partial preterist view. As long as premillennialists are the guiding voice in Western Christians, a type of self-fulfilling prophecy manifests in the world in which Christians have the spiritual authority to change. The future condition of the world is dependent upon Christians believing Biblical truth about who they are, what their mission is, and the ultimate result of their obedience to the commands of Christ revealed in the Scriptures.

What Did Jesus Say About His Kingdom?

It is important to recognize the things that Jesus said about His Kingdom because it gives us insight into His expectations for His Beloved. We also gain insight to the nature of His Kingdom and the way it would manifest itself in the lives of those who follow Jesus. There is a large amount of confusion and infighting in the greater Body of Christ on the nature of the Kingdom, its manifestation, the extends of its authority, and its experience lived out in the daily lives of Christians. It is unfortunate because Jesus said many things that should bring unity to His Church, if we understand the things He said about His Kingdom. At a basic level, we all need to acknowledge that Jesus is King; we are His subjects. Our main purpose in life is to bring Him as much glory as possible in our obedience to Him.

Whether it is in our workplace, family, service, play, and community, all things are for Him and done unto Him. Everything is sacred because He is the King of all things, the wonderful Designer of the world we live in.

One of the most interesting things that Jesus said about His Kingdom is that it is at hand, meaning that it was about to be inaugurated. Mark 4:17 says:

"From that time Jesus began to preach, saying, "Repent, for the kingdom of heaven is at hand [or has come near]."

When Western Christians think about repentance, we tend to contextualize that word is pertaining to sin, however, at the time Jesus said these words, He was speaking to a people who were expecting a Jewish Messiah to arrive on the scene who would be a great political leader in the archetype of King David. Certainly, repentance does include changing our minds concerning our conduct and agreeing with God that our sin needs forgiveness and mercy from Him in Christ, however, in this context, Jesus was asking the people to change their minds about the nature of the Kingdom of God. In their understanding, the ruling Messiah in the Kingdom of God, would be a political leader who would destroy the Roman occupation, cleanse the Temple, retake the Promised Land, and lead Israel to geopolitical prominence where the Gentile nations would submit to Messianic rule and pay tribute. They were expecting a physical Golden Age of everlasting goodness and prosperity.

This may have been the Messianic expectation in the mind of a First Century Jew, however, Jesus' Kingdom is spiritual first and will be manifested in the new creation order at His Second Coming. The Greek word for repent is **metanoe**, and its definition means to change one's mind for the better. Jesus demonstrated the nature of the Kingdom by connecting His description of the Kingdom of God by demonstrating spiritual power. Jesus' pattern of teaching about the Kingdom was both parabolic and demonstrative, rooted in spiritual concepts that speak to the inner life of the person. The happenings in the natural order all have an immaterial origin. Life, culture, and the organization of societies are the manifestation of the heart condition of the majority of the people or of their leader, if one is a tyrant. A cultural ethos is first a prevailing mindset before it ever becomes a reality. Jesus was teaching the people through signs and wonders that His Kingdom was discerned by the spiritual power rooted in love and goodness that one could observe. When Jesus cast out demons, He was freeing the person from the oppression of personalized evil. When Jesus healed the sick, He was demonstrating that His Kingdom healed the soul. Which is harder: Healing a body or healing a soul? We would all agree that healing human brokenness is a bigger miracle than that of the reordering and healing of cellular structures in the human body. At every season of Jesus' ministry, the Kingdom of God was connected to spiritual power that would ultimately renew the person first, and then through an obedient life as Christ follower, the world around them would be transformed.

The Kingdom of God is Parabolic

Jesus used parables to describe His Kingdom and to teach His followers about the nature of the Kingdom, its success in world history, and to encourage Christians of its ultimate triumph over the kingdoms of this age. Parables are wonderful because they communicate deep truths through metaphor, type, and symbol. Jesus was a Master at story-telling. He used the power of story to write us into His agenda for the world He created. Let's look at some the parables of Jesus that teach us about the Kingdom of God:

Sowing Seed — In Matthew 13, Jesus taught the Parable of the Sower. In this parable, Jesus called the gospel the "word of the kingdom." Jesus emphasized that everyone who would receive His word would bear fruit in their lives that demonstrated the "seed of the kingdom" was truly alive in them. Jesus gave examples of those who received the word but were unable to endure through either persecution or the pleasures and cares of this temporal life. The Parable of the Sower is an encouragement for Christians to personally seek to obey Jesus, love His teachings, and live a surrendered life unto Him. Jesus also said the Kingdom of God lives in the midst of us in Luke 17:21. This parable teaches us that our daily choices have eternal conse-quences. To summarize the Parable of the Sower, we would understand that the nature of the Kingdom of God lives from the inside of us and is demonstrated by the way we live to bring glory to the Lord. The harvest is all encompassing and includes everything from very personal things like our character to wide things like the global salvation of souls.

Leaven — In Luke 13:21, Jesus described the Kingdom of God like leaven. In this parable, Jesus uses the meta-phor of a woman who would work leaven throughout three measures of flour. The natural interpretation is as follows: 1) The world is the flour; 2) The woman is the Church; 3) The leaven is the Kingdom of God thoroughly mixed throughout the world causing the world to be influenced and transformed, just as leaven transforms dough. Therefore, Christians should be ex-pectant that throughout the course of the nations in world history, the Church of Jesus Christ will permeate and influence the entirety of the cultures. We will have success through the process of preaching the Gospel and being involved in every mover of society and cultural influence. The implications are far more reach-ing than simply planting churches in every nation of the world. Jesus prophesies a vision of slow success through the process of the faithfulness of Christians in all the accumulative ages of human history until

His return.

Mustard Seed — In Matthew 13:31, Jesus taught the Kingdom of God was like a mustard seed. If one has ever seen a mustard seed, they are indeed tiny and easily blown by the wind, as well as seemingly insignificant. Jesus was illustrating that like this tiny seed, His Church would start small. As it grew, it would be blown around by the wind of the Holy Spirit to eventually become a significant shelter for sinners to find God and His rest that accompanies the soul that is blessed by fellowship with God.

This parable teaches us that the Kingdom of God starts small and will eventually become a great entity that blesses the world. If we look at the trajectory of Church history, we can see that there were times of rapid growth with institutionalization that led to eras of corruption, reformations, and new movements that renew the faith. Looking back, we can see that though there are times of spiritual paralysis, the total sum of Church history speaks to a Global Church that is alive and larger today, doing more missions, planting more churches, and advancing in more nations of the world than it has since it began. The Church of Jesus Christ is advancing rapidly in the Global South and shrinking in the Global North. Perhaps the Church in the Global North needs to relearn the parables of Jesus and model its orthopraxy after the very successful Church in the Global South.

Seven Spheres Rising: Building Micro-Culture in Babylon

Fine Pearls — Again, in Matthew 13, Jesus teaches a short parable about the Kingdom of God being so priceless, that we would sell everything we have to possess it. Some believers in the Body of Christ have done just that yet, the general sense He is teaching is that the Kingdom of God is so important that we would pay any price to be close to God and to participate in its glory.

A Net — Jesus uses the typology of a net to describe the Kingdom of God/Heaven. Jesus teaches us that the Kingdom of God would net massive amounts of people in the harvest of humanity for God. The fish are people, and the net is the Gospel. The Church would constantly be fishing for souls as a central part of the expression of our faith. The expectation is that there would be an evangelistic edge to the Church that refreshes, renews, and restores itself with a harvest in each generation of humanity. One of the most heart-breaking observations in the West is the lack of young people being included in Church life. America's attachment to Dispensational Premillennialism has left the Church bankrupt of young adults because we selfishly believed we were the last generation. When eschatology overshadows Kingdom life, the victorious nature of Christian living is obscured by the zeal of apocalypse. It is hard to receive a message of apocalyptic vision when Jesus' vision was entirely different in its expectation for the future of His Bride.

In summary, as Western Christians return to an apostolic expression of the Gospel of the Kingdom, the result will be systemic change that is manifested through the collective of millions of Christians being real Christians on the earth. Just as it took decades of atheistic humanists to change the seven spheres of culture in the West, it will take decades of committed Christians following a First Century template of living to bring about the goodness of Jesus' dominion in the current world order. The true New World Order is not the vision of the globalists, but the expression of Jesus ruling the world through His Church through family, government, education, economy, arts, media, and religion. Christians in the West need to return to the foundation of the apostolic Gospel with the expectant hope that it would manifest into the world.

Chapter 4

Christian Social Engagement: A New Sociology

In the previous chapters, we have made the theological and philosophical arguments for Christians to be the guiding hand that brings goodness and blessing to the world. God designed societies to function through seven interdependent and overlapping spheres (Family, Education, Government, Economy, Arts, Media, and Religion) therefore, Christians have a responsibility to make their voices heard in culture and public policy. To remove the Christian voice from the common culture and public policy is to remove the wisdom and goodness of God from a people group. In the vacuum of Christianity in a culture, evil will increase because Christianity restrains sin. It is a "check" to hedonism, evil, and debauchery in a people group. Christianity brings a cultural awareness of right and wrong that influences a society to embrace the common good. Proverbs 29:18 says that when a people group does not have vision, they cast off restraint. In other words, the people become a law unto themselves.

There are dissenting Christian opinions on how involved Christians should be in the seven spheres of culture, and these dissenters cry out "Christian Nationalism" or some other red herring argument that removes the Church's influence from the common culture. By design, every culture has a religion, as even atheism is a theology. The dissenters who limit the Church only to the expression of love and grace completely miss the fundamental principles and teaching of Christianity. One cannot truly love without obedience or fidelity to the object of that love. One cannot extend grace unless an offense has occurred that has need to be covered. Sinning against one another and the need to forgive each other proves that Law is not divorced from love and grace. A rhetorical question to consider is who would you rather have lead a culture: those who fear God or those who have no fear of God? Those with no fear of God are unrestrained in the possibilities of how they might manage the people group they lead.

In this chapter, we will explore the types of Christian social engagement that make societies safe, closer to God, and prosperous.

GOVERNMENT — All societies are held together by their governments. Without government and law there are no boundaries by which the larger aggregate of the people is restrained from lawlessness in general.

The Christian sociologists see seven spheres of cultural intersection in every people group. These being Government, Family, Religion, Education, Economy, Arts/Entertainment, and Media. None of these spheres are independent of the others. All of these spheres intersect to create social change either for the common good, or the common bad. Government is the foundation that stabilizes the rest of the six spheres because it carries the policies that support the others. It is important to point out that the sphere of religion is the guiding worldview that energizes governmental action and all the other spheres of culture, but government animates the collective worldview in ways that are felt by the whole. For this reason, we will look at the sphere of government first.

All order originates in God. Genesis begins with God creating and ordering the cosmos according to His will. God is the first Governor and all other authorities or governments were created by Him and for Him. All governments mimic God's authority. Romans 13:1-7 is a clear explanation of the role of civil governments. They are to be first accountable to God, and then govern according to the common grace that God has revealed in humanity so that the other six spheres of culture are sustained in a way that is good for the collective. It is easy to see that governments that govern according to God's laws are better governments than those who disregard God and deny Him a place in the collective consciousness of their leaders.

Seven Spheres Rising: Building Micro-Culture in Babylon

History is filled with examples of tyranny and oppression that the ungodly mete out on the people they lead. History is also full of examples of governmental success when that government is godly. There are many examples in the Bible of the common good that godly leaders, kings, and governors bring to the aggregate of the people. An example of the governments of the Protestant West are the closest examples of the types of goodness that a government can give to its people, especially the example of the Constitutional Republic of the United States. The founding fathers of the American Republic may not have all been "born-again" Christians, but the prevailing worldview at the time was theistic at its root. The ideas they communicated all had their origins in the typologies found in the Scriptures and Classical Greek/Roman culture.

When we advocate for Christian engagement in the arena of government, we are focused on the goodness that the Christian worldview brings to the people through the Christian ethos. Christians bring an awareness to the government sphere that they are accountable to God for their decisions and personal conduct. They bring wisdom from the Scriptures that can be applied for the good of society. Romans 1:18-32 is a warning that when cultures depart from God they end up in a collective cultural mental illness that flows from the reprobate mind that has denied God. This is why it is imperative for Christians to run for political office, become educated in public policy, and most importantly vote in every election. One of the main drivers for the manifestation of the post-Christian America we are living in today is the Evangelical tendency to withdraw from participating in the political process.

Worldview and Eschatology

The two main drivers that influence Evangelical withdrawal from governmental and political engagement are worldview and eschatology. Many Christians in the West have a Platonic worldview that has divided the supernatural and the divine from natural order. Plato, Aristotle, and other classic Greek philosophers taught a cosmology of separation between the metaphysical world and natural world. A very elementary definition of this cosmology that Plato taught was called "form and matter." Form contained ideals like beauty, perfection, immortality, uncorrupted essence, and any higher thoughts of wisdom, etc. Form was separated from matter, which is base, subject to corruption, imperfect, and temporal. This type of cosmology was inculcated into Christianity through many theologians throughout the West from the Middle Ages to the Enlightenment. The net result was that far too many Christians in the West have separated God's central role in creation. The Biblical worldview places God at the center of all life lived in the human body, including marriage, conceiving and having a family, government, art, media, commerce, education, and worship. Modern Christians have inherited a worldview that makes a distinction between the secular and the spiritual. Throw in the confusion about separation of Church and state and we have Christians who think that they need to separate their political ideals from their faith in Christ. If one is truly a Christian, then God is at the center of his or her lived experience as a human. God has wisdom to guide every human experience and dimension of life. God has woven Himself into the fabric of life and cannot be separated from it.

The other influence that has produced the withdrawal from cultural engagement is Dispensational Premillennial Eschatology. The eschatological vision of premillennialism is a world that increasingly embraces satanic influence with a Church that grows cold, ultimately manifesting into an apocalyptic hell-scape that gets so bad that God must intervene. This is the prevailing eschatological view of Christians in America. This view is so entrenched in the Christian mindset regarding the future that it has robbed the Church of Her future because generational thinking is clouded by the near coming advent of the apocalypse. Of course, this is an oversimplification of the study of eschatology and worldview, but the essence of these statements is true. Modern Evangelicals have a worldview and eschatological problem that has paralyzed the American Church from participating in society for the common good of the people group we live with.

The bottom line is that Christians must reclaim

the Biblical worldview by getting involved in every dimension of leadership in government such as public service, policy involvement, elected office, and city planning. Our absence has allowed evil to prosper, and our culture has become post-Christian in its worldview as a result. Our entire society has become a mostly a hedonistic economic marketplace that has departed from its accountability to God. The example of Rome is about to repeat itself in 5G. In the opinion of this writer, it is better to preserve and reform than to rebuild.

FAMILY — The family was the first cultural institution that God blessed humanity with. In the beginning of Genesis, one of the greatest mandates the LORD God gave to humanity was to be fruitful and multiply. The command was not to simply reproduce, but to create a lifelong experience of love and nurture that gives society stability. Marriage is the primary mover of sustaining the greatest good in individuals with its highest effect of producing the greatest good in a people group. The Scriptures teach many things about family, from how we should view marriage to how we should raise children and care for one another. It could be stated that society's modern challenges, from crime to corruption, all find their origins in the disfunction of the family.

The family sphere is the greatest opportunity

for Christians to speak to the culture. It is universal that every person would desire a good family. When a family is ordered after God's desire and vision for it, then happiness and prosperity increases. The Scriptures have wisdom for every dimension of family: how husbands and wives are to love one another and how they are to raise their children. Family is our first government with parents acting as the executives, and children learning to respect their authority which translates to good behavior in their young adult years. Family encompasses the foundation from which children live the rest of their lives. Parents teach children every life skill and when these life skills revolve around God, then parents bless their children and therefore, bless society as whole.

Christian engagement in the sphere of family is to prioritize God, marry well and raise children to love God. We are to teach our children their identity in Christ, encourage them in their giftings and calling, and thus lead a new revival in the family sphere. Too many of us have been a partner to divorce and have made poor choices or have sacrificed our children on the altar of ministry and have not invested in the next generation. Unfortunately, the current Church is downstream from culture, and sadly, the Church mirrors the systemic brokenness of the family. It will take some time to cast new vision for marriage and family and for the family reformation to manifest its goodness.

The atheist modern-day Left understands that to institute socialist collectivism, the family unit needs to be redefined with the traditional family dismantled. The public policies of no-fault divorce, LGBTQ+ lifestyles, polyamory, bigamy, pornography and any other deviation from the traditional family structure God designed empowers the State to become the progenitor, and not the father and mother. Any family unit that is unhitched from the awareness of God's authority is vulnerable to the unnatural template pushed by the atheist modern Left. The spiritual warfare surrounding the family sphere is intense and it is necessary for Christian leaders to recognize that systemic problems are symptomatic of that spiritual war. We will leave this sphere for now and spend more time speaking to the revival and reformation of the Family sphere in Chapter Seven.

RELIGION — In terms of shaping the consciousness of a culture, what the people believe to be true about God (or gods), in the general sense, determines the goodness that that culture experiences. Every culture is based upon canon. Canon is typically the sacred texts, oral histories, fable, literature and mythologies that give the culture its unique identity and expression. Religion is the genesis of canon and cultures that possess the canon of the God of the Bible have enjoyed the most prosperity, technological advancement, and the nicest living conditions than all others. These nations have benefitted by applying God's wisdom to every-day life and have reaped the harvest of an aggregate people who are aware and accountable to the God of the Bible.

Cultures whose canon is far from God suffer the most poverty and war. They have the least amount of technological advancement and live in more cultural chaos than those whose canon is the Bible. World history is evidence that when people groups use the Bible as their canon prosper in every way. The West is now departing from its founding canon of Holy Scripture and what will emerge will either be a neo-pagan or a humanist atheistic canon. It is not far reaching to think that *Star Wars*, *Hunger Games*, or some other cultural mythology will replace the Judeo-Christian ethos of the West. Perhaps the new canon may be an AI atheistic religion of trans-humanism where we attempt to download consciousness and live forever as AI holographic avatars of our former human selves. The global elite would love to shift humanity from carbon to silicone because the endgame is depopulation and control. The desire to transcend our lived reality is hardwired into humanity by God. Humanity will never leave the sphere of religion with even atheism offering a silicone immortality with the rise in AI technology.

The Church of Jesus Christ in the West desperately needs to become evangelistic and lead the people to the true religion of the God of the Bible. So many of us are afraid of the soft persecution of social media that we self-censor the tenets of our faith and therefore empower an anti-Biblical canon of pop-culture to become the predominant religion and canon. For Christians to engage the sphere of religion, we must plant churches, preach the Apostolic gospel, and teach Christians to become devoted disciples of Jesus Christ.

Forsaking and Consequential Judgment

The whole witness of the Bible teaches us the ways that God deals with individuals and nations. There are many instances where God judges individuals and nations based upon their willingness to acknowledge Him and His authority. Just a few Biblical examples are Nebuchadnezzar, Ahab, and Manasseh. These leaders all willingly chose to disobey God's rightful place of authority and God dealt with them in the context of consequential judgment. Consequential judgment is simply God responding to their personal choices and honoring those choices by determining the level of judgment in order to turn them back to Himself. In Nebuchadnezzar's case, he confessed faith in God and at least submitted to His authority. In Ahab's case, God gave grace to Ahab when he repented, however, God did judge Ahab directly for leading Israel astray to worship idols instead of seeking their one true God. Manasseh was so evil that the LORD judged him by judging the whole nation of Judah.

Manasseh's example is chilling in that a leader can set the course of a nation towards forsaking judgment. Forsaking judgment is when the LORD leaves that nation to its own devices and the whole aggregate of the people suffer because God cannot and will not partner with their collective sin. A nation that was founded on the canon of Scripture and had worshipped God but chooses to depart from Him is indeed in danger of both the consequential and forsaking judgment of God. This is precisely why American Evangelicals need to disciple America to return to God. (For more about these judgments of God, you can find my book, *"Diakrino: How is God Judging the World Today?"* on Amazon.)

EDUCATION — The knowledge base of a people is the foundation for their collective wisdom, technology, art, literature, and public policy. Education is downstream from the canon of that culture because it provides the epistemological framework from which they teach their children. The observation currently is that American culture is malevolent in its manifestation and is hurting the collective consciousness of the people. At almost every metric, America is failing morally, economically, socially, and culturally. Our leaders are corrupt globalist grifters who promote every kind of behavior that is against the Law of God. The average American high school graduate has little knowledge of the founding of the United States, its Declaration of Independence or its Constitution. The modern education system is a deliberate departure from the foundation of God and Country to the foundation of godlessness, emotions, and sexual deviance in every form.

There cannot be any education without God because within God is all knowledge, wisdom, and understanding. God is Creator: We live, move, and have our being inside of His creation. Therefore, any education that denies God is really no education at all. This is where Christians miss the importance of educating their children. The Bible is clear that it is the parents' primary responsibility to educate their children. It is not the responsibility of the state or any other entity. Parents alone are charged with overseeing, managing, and teaching their children to love God, enjoy His creation, and glorify Him through their lives. For Christians to become great leaders, policy makers, and cultural influencers, we must begin to educate our children in a very different way. Education is the North Star of any culture. Education sets the trajectory of a generation either towards God or away from Him. In next chapter, we will explore the desperately needed educational reformation that God is calling Christian leaders and parents into.

ECONOMY — The Bible has always promoted economy based on the free market of the exchange of goods and services. From the earliest times recorded in Genesis, we find people who were skilled in a variety of ways and giftings that God gave them, either collectively or individually. These people traded with one another for the common good. The book of Proverbs is a master class on weights and measures, and ethics in trade. In it are found many verses that teach us trade, good character, and a strong work ethic brings prosperity to people, both collectively and individually.

It is important to note that the Proverbs also include the supernatural action of God regarding trade, economy, and business ethics. For those who trade and do business in the right way, God opens the storehouses of blessing and favor over their lives. The Proverbs teach that God has a way to do business that releases His blessing and goodness in a business-person's life. Understanding these things gives the Christian businessperson a distinct advantage in the marketplace. Christian businesspeople approach the marketplace from a position of strength, wisdom, faith, and favor from God because they know who they are and Whose they are.

The 3 Pillars of Biblical Economics

Biblical economies benefit everyone because they stand on three pillars. The first pillar of Biblical economics is that every person participating in the economy is participating from the foundation of their intrinsic value in God. When people participate in the marketplace from their God-given skill, craft, wisdom, and Spirit-inspired ideas, the grace to prosper in God's favor and blessing opens wide for that person. The first pillar also stands on the altruistic vision that each person who participates in the economy blesses those around them because they are exercising their God-given skill and service. As the Reformation scholars and theologians in the 16th Century stated, *"Work is worship."* Martin Luther said:

> *"The best commendation of any work is to know that one has done the work that God has given him well and that God is pleased with his effort."*

The first pillar of Biblical economics simply states that we all have a gift from God to bless the people in our communities. Biblical economics is symbiotic, interdependent, and altruistic in its trade of goods and services.

The second pillar of Biblical economics is applied wisdom and creativity. Applied wisdom in business begins with good character that flows from having reverence for God. Having reverence for God means obeying His Word and living life from the revealed wisdom of the Word of God. This second pillar includes prayer, the expression of faith, obedience to God's moral law, and moving in the inspiration of the Holy Spirit. It becomes the "law" of the marketplace by regulating cheats, scams, and dishonesty because those who operate in these marketplace injustices lose both their credibility and their standing before God. This pillar of Biblical economics is natural and supernatural. If one conducts their lives in a way that aligns with God's likes and dislikes, then that person has favor with both God and man. We should note that money is portable power and money is an amplifier in a person's life. If we are dishonest with a little, we will be even more dishonest with a lot. Money is an amplifier in the sense that it amplifies a person's ability to either be altruistic with it, or it amplifies a person's base human nature.

The third pillar of Biblical economics is generosity through giving tithes, offerings, and philanthropy. Accumulated wealth is always focused on two aspects of its power. The first aspect is to build generational wealth that empowers future generations to prosper in the ways that God has gifted them. True marketplace freedom is to live one's life as directed by God based on their ability. Building generational wealth builds a foundation for the generations that follow to begin to form a place of blessing. The second aspect is to build and maintain social actions and relationships that advance God's Kingdom in our lifetimes. These societal institutions are schools, libraries, hospitals, trade guilds, political action groups, charities, and ministries/churches.

This third pillar of Biblical economics is the one most neglected by Christians because they fail to understand the three pillars of Biblical economics, yet these three pillars are found throughout Scripture. They teach us that wealth is power, and that power is sustained by generosity, tithes, offerings, and philanthropic action. One of main reasons Christianity in the West has lost its influence is that it's has denied the three pillars of Biblical economics and only focused on building the narrow vision of church buildings and funding missionaries. It has failed to build institutions that create culture, leaving these responsibilities for the state to provide. May Christians today get motivated to build micro-cultures that would become culture once again!

ARTS & CREATIVITY/ENTERTAINMENT — One of the most beautiful manifestations of Imago Dei in humanity is art and creativity. God is the Master Artist Who, as Creator, possesses the most creative, masterful mind in the universe. The wonderful manifold giftings of craftsmanship, fine art, writing, creativity, and design all flow from Him. In the opinion of this author, all the disciplines of engineering and architecture are included in the arts and entertainment sphere. We love beautifully designed products and cars that not only work well but are also aesthetically pleasing. Arts and Creativity speak the loudest about humanity reflecting the God who created them. So much is communicated non-verbally when we experience art, design, and music. One could say the greatest mover in a culture is its expressions of the arts.

In the past, the Christian West was on the leading edge of producing works of beauty from fine arts and music, to the design of cities and its infrastructure. Currently, the realm of arts and creativity has moved away from beauty and has embraced dark themes. The arts and entertainment industry in America has exported wholesale rebellion against God around the world and debauched at least the last three generations of people. Every area of arts and creativity has devolved towards evil and it is communicating the darkness of our national soul. There have been Christian attempts at arts and creativity, but these have been so religiously themed and low quality that they have been of no consequence to the wider culture. We have simply created arts and entertainment that is geared only for our Christian sub-culture. The coming revolution in arts and entertainment is to not produce "Christian art" but to produce art that is made by Christians. We have missed the power of storytelling, and by our pseudo-Puritanism, we have discouraged artists and creatives from pursuing their passions due to our religious isolation.

Christians have the best stories to tell, and we have access to the highest, most creative Mind through the Holy Spirit dwelling in us! Our opportunity now is to build parallel competing communities of arts and entertainment. If we do them well, we will watch our cultural influence grow. The arts and entertainment sphere does not need to be overtly Christian to be great and influential. It need only be authentic, speaking to the issues of the human heart. The arts steer a culture toward a direction of either collective goodness or the consequential and forsaking judgment of God.

MEDIA — Today's media is cursed as it denies free speech principles. Free speech is a Biblical principle due to the fact that free speech defends the truth. Truth in the Christian worldview is inviolable because God is truth and all truth comes from Him. Truth is not subjective; truth is within the boundaries of God's moral law. Journalism today is based on political and social agendas that deny God as the Source of truth, the Arbiter of truth, and the Revealer of truth. The modern mainstream media does not defend free speech. It is not concerned with unbiased reporting or the analysis of facts and happenings in the world today.

Biblical journalism is journalism that seeks truth and defends freedom of speech. The Bible is the most honest free speech Book in existence. Every Biblical hero or heroine's life is told in the context of their glories, as well as their weaknesses, shortcomings and sins. If societies do not have free speech, then they exist in pockets of conspiracies that defend and insulate themselves from real accountability. When media outlets and the marketplace of ideas (social media platforms) limit speech, then they limit truth that often expresses itself in revealing conspiracies and propaganda. There is one media principle that cannot be violated: *The truth always comes to light.* Free speech makes that light of truth shine brighter for people to see.

Christians have a wonderful opportunity to build new media that will not violate, but defend truth telling and free speech. As these media platforms emerge, they will build viewership quickly because people appreciate being told the straight truth. This means that these new media outlets cannot and will not push a political agenda but look at all things through objectivity and integrity. These new media entities will certainly need to uphold a Biblical worldview. They will need to tell their audience when they are reporting facts or offering opinions. Our modern mainstream media is pushing opinion, ideologies, and social constructs. They are pundits, not journalists.

To summarize, Christians are needed in every sphere and expression of culture and society because together we bring the influence of God's wisdom, character, and blessings to the common culture. As we have looked at Christian social action, we can see that each one of us plays a role in these interdependent spheres of society to advance God's Kingdom and the knowledge of God in a people group. When Christians guide a culture, we preserve that culture making it prosperous, safe, and more just. We bring an abundance of benevolence to people when we understand that our lives transcend our own. Our lives reverberate through our neighborhoods, cities, states, and country. It is time to leave the negativity behind us and become the solution. We certainly have the mandate from Jesus Himself to do this in Matthew 28:18-20.

Chapter 5

Educating World-Changers for Systemic Counter Revolution

T he foundation for a future culture change, begins with the founding of educational institutions that are focused on producing world changers. The modern mode of education in the United States is primarily directed at humanistic and atheistic visions for the direction of the common culture. The theistic (or Biblical) worldview is not even allowed to be taught by law. The concepts of creationism, moral law, grammar, logic and rhetoric have been replaced by godlessness that trains our children to not think about God but to live from base human instincts. It never ceases to amaze me when Christian parents deliver their children to satanic indoctrinators Monday through Friday and then wonder why their children leave the faith, deny God, live ungodly life-styles, and vote for public policies that advance sin in society. Sadly, they seem unaware of the social decay our government-operated public schools are producing. On the other hand, Christian education has become big business and a major source of profit for religious organizations. The modern mode of Christian education is almost untouchable for the average family in the modern American economy with average tuition per child of $1,000+ per month.

This chapter seeks to inspire a new path of Christian education that is revolutionary and bold. In this chapter, we will look at alternative avenues of education that hopefully inspires and launches a neo-renaissance in American Christian education. An affordable, quality education is a potent form of social justice considering that being uneducated or uninformed feeds the poverty cycle. Prosperous people are not easily controlled.

Parents, Our Primary Teachers

In Deuteronomy 6:7, we find instructions from the LORD to parents about how to raise their children. It reads:

> *"You shall teach them diligently to your children, and shall talk of them when you sit in your house, and when you walk by the way, and when you lie down, and when you rise."*

The context of this verse is the law of God, which contains all the necessary information to live life well and to prosper both individually and collectively. The

Bible is clear that parents have the responsibility to raise their children to first love God, then to respect themselves in the context of the law. They must teach them to respect others and live in a way that brings goodness to society and glory to God. If God is the origin of all knowledge and wisdom, then learning to know Him is the first teaching we should receive. One cannot be truly educated without first knowing the Teacher. This implies that parents are responsible for every aspect of their child's education which also includes self-care, obedience, social graces, discipline, stature, and formal learning. Parents are the curators and protectors of their child's development. Christian parents are responsible for shepherding their children into the Christian faith to become Christians themselves. It is ignorance to hold the position of "we will let them choose their path" when Scripture teaches otherwise. There are many other verses in Scripture that teach us that parents bear the sole responsibility for training their children in the way of the LORD. Since the Bible educates us in almost everything, we should be teaching them the Scriptures from the earliest start.

A thorough knowledge of the Bible empowers a person to live well, enjoy fellowship with God, and prosper in every area of life. Christian parents separate education from religion when education is religious training. Every subject that can be taught in school from civics, to history, to the STEM disciplines all have their Genesis in God's creation and Biblical cosmology and worldview. Many Christian parents today divide education and religious training. Monday through Friday they send their children to public school and then on Sunday the children learn about God, oftentimes only once or twice a month. This is not the Biblical pattern of education. All life revolves around God and to divide our relationship with God from education is a serious misstep of the modern parent. The first revelation of the coming educational renaissance is that parents are the primary, God-ordained, authoritative teacher.

To support this idea, in Massachusetts the Early American colonists passed the Old Deluder Satan Act of 1647. In summary, it stated that education existed to teach children the Scriptures in order to counter Satan's spiritual warfare against humanity and, in that, learning the Scriptures made society better as a whole and kept future generations from error. In addition to this, Samuel Adams wrote:

> *"Let Divines, and Philosophers, Statesmen, and Patriots unite...by impressing the Minds of Men with the importance of educating their little boys, and girls...in short of leading them in the Study, and Practice of the exalted Virtues of the Christian system."*

At the time our nation was founded, our education system was a tuition-free Christian education that was disseminated through homeschooling groups or churches.

Education Is Not a Business Model _______

As mentioned previously, all cultures are built on canon. Canon is the collection of that culture's sacred texts, literature, common mythologies, and heroic histories. Because the founding of the United States was primarily Christian in nature, its Christian ethos was built upon the canon of the Holy Bible. With this canon and the collection of Western literary works, the nation prospered with prosperity, ingenuity, creative inventions, prosperous markets, and industries. Education was tuition-free, and that education translated into social transformation. With all the chatter about social justice in our world today, it would be true to say that authentic social justice is a good education.

Modern Christian education has developed into a business model that can be very lucrative, especially in today's educational environment. The modern day societal and cultural pain points are great marketing opportunities for Christian schools however, we should search our souls and ask ourselves about the *"why"* of Christian education. It begs to ask, *"Is Christian education first about equipping and releasing world changers ready to reimagine the world into something that gives God glory?"* Or *"Is Christian education a lucrative business that capitalizes on social pain points with the added benefit of teaching children the basics about God?"*

Christian educators who are forward-thinking will seize the opportunity to create low cost or tuition-free schools that train children in liberal arts centered around God. This type of thinking is a radical departure from the traditional approach to Christian education. Instead of business, it becomes a missional effort and an investment into the future that will seed the culture with Christian influencers. If Christians can rethink education, then we can very quickly turn a nation towards God and enjoy His benevolent and providential goodness towards its people.

Christian Philanthropy and Mission _________

The alternative business model for Christian schools could be a two-fold effort of funding. The first step is to begin to reframe the *"why"* of education. When we begin to see education as a social and cultural investment, then the purpose of Christian education becomes the spreading of the Gospel and the Kingdom of God in its vision and mission. This means that funding for Christian schools becomes a philanthropic priority, as well as a Missions budget priority of the local church.

For instance, the Southern Baptist Convention raised 196.1 million dollars to fund the Lottie Moon

Missionary fund that disperses this money into international missions. In fact, Christian missions giving is about 52 billion dollars annually and in 2022, all Christian global giving totaled $53 trillion dollars (*missionfrontiers.org*). The American Evangelical Church disperses billions of dollars across the globe but fails to fund low-cost or tuition-free Christian schools in every community in America. It is time re-prioritize our Missions funds and spend them locally, funding the mission of Christian education which preserves Christianity in its host nation and will ultimately bless that nation in the long run.

This vision for funding Christian schools is indeed radical, but the gravity of the American situation is so serious that it is time to start providing solutions to education and stop complaining about it. Think of the many evangelistic opportunities low-cost or tuition-free Christian schools would provide for local churches. Many unbelievers will place their children in those schools thus opening the door of opportunity to bring the goodness of God to those families. Think about the many single parents who need a solution for their child's education and all the good that can come from educating children who are disadvantaged. I am advocating for a recall of international Christian missions giving in order to turn those funds toward our own communities to fund Christian schools. We can then fund both mission fields when our priorities are aligned with God's priorities, which begins with educating children correctly. Unfortunately, many (not all) Christian international mission trips are religious colonizing efforts or religious feel good vacations, if we are honest. Overall, a country's destiny is determined by the efforts of the indigenous population, not the missionaries. Missionaries may be sent to seed the Gospel, but it is only sustained by local communities of Christians living for Jesus in the seven spheres of culture. The common culture in the Global South is now more Christian than it is in the West. There is not an urgent need for Western missionaries to spend their efforts in the Global South, rather the West needs the Global South to send missionaries to help return us to the Gospel of the Kingdom. Today in America, however, we have an urgent need for children to be educated in the Christian worldview and moral law with excellence in academics.

How Should We Educate?

The coming reformation of Christian education is not confined only to funding. A whole new approach of shifting from institutional pedagogies to communal pedagogies of learning is necessary. In the early years of America, education took place in the community of combined grades with group learning. The teacher acted as facilitator, coach, and mentor to the students. Teachers empowering individualism, respect for others, and meritorious reward for high achievement have been lost in the modern education pedagogy.

Instead, what is happening currently in education is a movement of social engineering rather than empowering students with critical thinking skills and logic. This is by design in the interest of secular humanists and socialist cultural engineers who desire a monolithic plebiscite class that can be controlled by the type of social conformity that produces group think, or the hive-mind. When the whole culture is guided by social conformity and social pressure then the consolidation of wealth by the few is possible. Only education that is structured around grammar, rhetoric, and logic can inoculate itself from the modern hive-mind education system in the American government public schools.

The Christian reformed alternative for education is to have combined grades that learn in community together utilizing the teachers as learning facilitators, mentors, and coaches all within the context of Christian discipleship. The Scriptures speak to every aspect of human life and learning therefore, the Christian worldview can be woven into every subject. Christians need never be afraid of science or scientific advancement because the STEM disciplines support the belief in God. Every subject that a student learns about is an exploration into God's great creation and His interaction with it. These class sizes will be small with the reinforcement of positive and emotionally healthy behavior between students. The Christian worldview differs from the humanistic worldview in that it sees all people as made in God's image who possess intrinsic value as an individual. It is very important for Christian education to focus on developing the student's emotional IQ in addition to excellence in learning.

Lastly, this Christian education reformation views shorter school days as necessary to maintain quality family life. In the typical school (Christian or public), students are away at school for 8 hours a day only to have homework that eats up precious family time when they get home. If students are involved in extra-curricular activities, their day ends late at night only to wake up tired the next day. Truly, the lack of family connection at the end of the school day is a disadvantage to parents and students alike. We desperately need a new model of learning that prevents student burnout, robbing a family of the precious time they have to connect with their children after school. Reducing the hours of study to maintain the student's focus while working through each subject and then assigning homework only if one cannot complete his/her tasks is the answer to this issue. We are advocating for a total rethinking of education in every metric from classroom structure, amount of study hours, teacher roles, new approaches to each subject, and moral and ethical training of the student. The American education system is mostly failing, and our global competitors across the world will at some point eclipse the West if there is not a drastic change in academic pedagogy.

Empowering World Changers ___________

When the focus of a student's education is empowering them to discover their God given gifts, talents, and passions, then that student is being positioned to thrive and to enjoy a life focused on what they were made for. The highest condition of blessedness for every human being is to bring God glory through their lives. As the new Christian education reformation begins, students will no longer be part of the socially engineered monolith. They will become the individuals God created them to be, having a specific potential purpose from which to live their lives. Every vocation in a society is valuable because we are all interdependent. Too much focus in the local church is placed on how one serves the church when the focus should really be on how one serves society. Work is worship. Students who are taught that the world is holy because God created it will be prepared to thrive and prosper no matter if they become a plumber, teacher, mechanic, attorney, medical doctor, or scientist. Each person is given grace for a specific purpose/destiny in this life. It is a great tragedy to live a life divorced from our God-given passion and gifting. We owe it to our children to raise them to know these things.

When Christians become focused on producing people who love God, love life, and have vision for their specific role in the seven spheres of culture, then Christian education becomes a powerful force for cultural revolution that cannot be resisted. We should have a *"Discover Your Destiny"* class each year for ninth to twelfth grade students to help them discover their unique path they were given from God to prepare them for their future. This powerful self-discovery could then be empowered by making time and opportunity for those students to experiment with their passion and map out the most expedient ways to enter that trade or profession. It is always wise to pastor a student's talents and giftings so they can live great lives with purpose. There are many young people who graduate high school with no vision for their lives or pathway for entering the work force. This trend has produced prolonged adolescence and the failure of many young men and women to become successful early enough in life to get married, buy houses or build assets. It is time for a radically new education reform that will break the cultural death spiral that the West is currently experiencing. It is time to educate and empower our future world changers so that they do not become victims to the globalist vision for collectivism and progressive social change in the West.

Chapter 6

Micro-Culture Becomes Culture__

The only admirable thing about the Progressive Left in America is their understanding of social action and commitment to cultural change. The modern Conservative Right in America is postured in a defensive position seeking to "conserve" or prevent change in the social fabric and culture of the nation. The Left is focused on changing cultural norms, and the Right is focused on slowing or stopping cultural change that is imposed by the Left. The problem here is that change is an inevitability in God's world, so the focus of godly change should be the strategy of implementing God's wisdom and solutions into the world. The Left is carrying a vision to fundamentally change the West in ways that exclude God, deny His authority, and erase His moral and ethical commands in Scripture in order to remake the West on the canon of Humanism and Atheism. Christians should be less focused on preserving the status quo, and more focused on counter-revolutionary ideas and actions that would move the West towards God. Christians who are concerned and called to culture change can learn many things from the Progressive Left. This chapter will focus on actionable cultural change and strategic thinking that eclipses the modern reactionary Right that seeks to preserve, but not reform.

Systemic Change

Interestingly, systemic change does not start at the highest levels of society. The status quo of a culture is maintained and enforced at the highest levels of each societal/cultural sphere: Family, Government, Religion, Education, Media, Economy, and Arts/Entertainment. Systemic change is always seeded at the local and grassroots level by those who have vision for a culture. The modern Progressive Left understands this and through approximately the last 70 years, the Progressive Left has been able to create grassroots and local concentrations of aggregate agreement that has been seeded and now sits at the highest levels of the seven spheres of culture. The Progressive Left began a countercultural movement through maintaining committed vision, political activism, micro-culture building, and institutional infiltration that has now won the culture war in the West, particularly America.

The modern Right is now postured in a position of defense, trying to hang on to a very slim margin of cultural Christianity and Western Canon rather than realizing it has lost the culture war. The way forward is to admit the loss of the culture war and begin to commit to a long-term vision of building a break-away culture concentrated in local communities with like-minded people ready to play the long game of establishing micro-cultures that become culture.

The Progressive Left seeded their humanistic and atheistic vision for America by concentrating their efforts locally in San Francisco and Chicago. These micro-cultural centers have become the culture that influences almost every aspect of American social fabric. If one chooses to study San Francisco and Chicago, they will find the systematic founding, culti-vation, and infiltration of cultural institutions with the ideas that now guide the West. Homosexual marriage, transsexual identity, socialist/labor movements, athe-ism, humanism, and the counter-cultural shift of moving away from Christianity was all seeded in these two cities. In fact, the most influential leftist politi-cians who have affected the most cultural change in America have come from these two cities. No longer can the Left "rage against the machine" – they are the machine. Biblical Christianity is the new punk rock.

Not all of the West has been conquered by the Progressive Left, so we have hope. There are still many areas where cultural Christianity survives, however, the cultural Christian hangover is no longer the North Star of the culture. It is time to start local new micro-cultural communities that build the momentum for becoming culture. To be clear: we are not advocating for a return to "what was lost." We are proposing a new way forward where a culture becomes more Christian without the racism and inequality of opportunity as in the past expressions of American society. Many of those on the Right want to go back; we want to go forward. We want to reform culture with a return to the founding ideals of America, not its institutional failures that gave room for the palatability of Leftist influences in the common culture.

Seeding A Micro-Culture

Micro-cultures are seeded at the grassroots and local levels over a period of years, even decades. This is the barrier for Christian reformation in the seven spheres of culture. Unfortunately, the modern Evangelical Christian has been conditioned to think "Apocalyptically" and not "Kingdom Now" in their vision for the world or their nation. American Evangelicals need a theological and worldview detox in order to see that investing in society and participating in building a new common culture is a worthwhile effort. After all, God is still the Sovereign over His creation, and He is still interested in the fulfillment of Matthew 28:18-20. When Christians can detach from the societal implications of Dispensational Theology and the escapism of the rapture theory, then the work of micro-culture building can begin. The preeminent step in seeding a micro-culture is a theological one that begins in the pulpit.

Seeding micro-cultures begins with a commitment to start small and give your life to the long and inglorious work of living for a vision you will most likely not see manifest in your lifetime. This is a Biblical concept. Hebrews 11:39 says:

"And all these, though commended through their faith, did not receive what was promised."

The writer of Hebrews was referring to the great hall of faith, the men and women like Abraham and Rahab who were moved by faith in the long vision God had given them, but it was not fulfilled in their lifetimes. The long work of cultural reformation is one that is incremental and can only be discerned by looking back over the years and decades. It is a generational work that requires the adventurous spirit of a pioneer married to the perseverance of a prize fighter.

The one thing that needs attention is that the atheistand unbiblical Left do not have the anointing or mandate from God, nor the power of His word to sustain their endeavors. Christians are the only people who are commanded and given the grace to reshape the world to conform to Jesus Christ. All other authorities, powers, rulers, and social institutions are accountable to Him. The modern Left are usurpers when compared to the legitimate authority that Christians possess in Christ.

Seven Spheres Rising: Building Micro-Culture in Babylon

The next strategic step to begin seeding a micro-culture is to form community around a local church. Local churches are by nature generational institutions that are natural hubs for ministering to local communities and launching grassroots culture change efforts. When a local church moves into the seven sphere vision for cultural change, then that local church can begin to make room for the development of the local strategic planning and empowerment to seed and found a micro-culture. Local churches can start Christian schools and support networks of professionals and tradespeople. They can run members for local office, and minister to the needs and challenges of a local community. As these relatively easy and effective micro-cultures are built, then the founding of more impactful culture-influencing institutions can be laid on this foundation.

The next level of strategic micro-culture building is the founding of political Super-PACs, philanthropic societies, trade apprenticeships, media outlets, Schools of Creativity, and Liberal Arts universities. This level of collaboration and action requires more commitment and concentrated wealth to accomplish the transition from micro-culture to culture. The barrier to this level of strategic engagement with the culture is theological (as previously mentioned) and having a poverty mindset in the Church. Most American Evangelicals have been inculcated into the Monastic thinking that drives the poverty mindset into the

Church. Unfortunately, the hangover from Monastic movements of the past in Christian history is the prevailing thought that poverty is holiness and simplicity is spiritual. This is simply not true. Wealth and resources are Kingdom principles that, when managed with Holy Spirit inspired wisdom and revelation, are necessary tools for advancing God's agendas at the highest levels of the seven spheres of culture. The failed institutions of Harvard, Princeton, and Yale Universities were all founded to advance God's Kingdom in America. These institutions lost their vision and have fallen into the hands of the Progressive Left who have blasphemed God and defiled the original missions of these universities. The blind truly are leading the blind, as illumination only comes from our creator God.

The founding of institutions of higher learning are very necessary to seed culture with creativity, arts, news media, music, literature, and leadership that becomes the culture. Societies and cultures that are closer to conforming to God's laws are safer, more prosperous, and more stable. This is the way forward to creating a new Renaissance in the West. There are always flash points where people congregate in significant numbers to effect global change. Think about the radical transformations of Geneva, Switzerland and various American Colonies that became the predominant producer of thoughts and goods that transformed the world. The American Colonies emerged from a backwoods micro-culture to become global culture as they embraced God, followed His blueprints for building a society, and reaped His blessing. Possibly, the next backwoods to emerge as a global leader in Christian reformation may be located in the Global South, or it may emerge from the fly over country of rural America.

The X Factor: Spiritual Warfare Prayer ______

One of the neglected aspects of cultural reformation in the seven spheres of culture is prayer and spiritual warfare. In the Christian worldview, the spiritual realm animates the natural realm. Christian reformers realize that prayer is the necessary component of all action in the seven spheres of culture. At every juncture of the colonial American journey, our leaders all engaged in prayer and committed their ways to God. For example, Benjamin Franklin prayed in 1747:

> *"May the God of Wisdom, Strength and Power, the Lord of the Armies of Israel, inspire us with Prudence in this Time of Danger; take away from us all the Seeds of Contention and Division, and unite the Hearts and Counsels of all of us, of whatever Sect or Nation, in one Bond of Peace, Brotherly Love, and generous Publick Spirit; May he give us Strength and Resolution to amend our Lives, and remove from among us every Thing that is displeasing to him; afford us his most gracious Protection, confound the*

Designs of our Enemies, and give Peace in all our Borders, is the sincere Prayer of A Trades-man of Philadelphia."

Notice the spiritual warfare components in this prayer of Benjamin Franklin. Mr. Franklin seeks God's favor, realizes there are spiritual enemies that sow division and contention and natural enemies that stand against God's purposes for the people of the American Colonies. This type of prayer is non-existent in our current leaders today, and the result is the descendant path of the West. We are no longer ascendant as a nation because we our leaders have forsaken the place of spiritual warfare prayer. This is not an isolated example of the centrality of prayer in our nation's history. There are so many examples but it is not expedient for this abbreviated work to mention them. Fortunately, there are many great resources to equip the Church today in spiritual warfare prayer so we will not spend too much effort making the point. The main point is that there is no effectual or lasting cultural influence without the many prayers of righteous people. Prayer and spiritual warfare prayer are the X factor in cultural reformation. There can be no victory in the long game of cultural reformation without prayer. Truly, the future belongs to the intercessors.

Social Media: The Wild Card _______________

One of the variables in culture change is the influence

of social media. So far, social media has cultivated the worst in humanity in terms of selfishness, division, the promotion of sexual degradation of our culture, and the control of populations and generations of people defined the by "likes" or "dislikes." Social media has become a spiritual and cultural Wild West. It has also become a warped town crier in a warped town square where unpopular opinions and ideas are censored and/or cancelled. That is because the social engineers at play understand that regulating free speech is necessary to regulate and contain truth.

On the other hand, the wonderful untapped potential of social media is that it amplifies micro-culture because the whole world becomes local with a cell phone in our hands. There are tremendous opportunities and benefits for content creation that is excellent if it is deployed strategically. It remains to be seen if social media can be leveraged in a way that brings cultural reformation to the West. So far, its net results have been negative on its impact on societal and mental health. Social media may be a spiritual and cultural Wild West but is also affords strategic thinking. Christians now have the opportunity to create news media organizations, new targeted content on fields of interest like family, marriage, trades, professions, hobbies, film, and politics. Possibly the answer to leveraging social media in the cultural reformation is moderation and excellence.

Wisdom Proved Right by Her Children ______

Good living is attractive and contagious. The seven needs of the human heart are all hardwired into the human experience from God. These needs are significance, service, acceptance, celebration, accomplishment, happiness, and safety. Every person on earth craves these seven experiential dimensions in their lives, with or without a relationship with God. The Scriptures are clear: when a person's life is lived in the context of Biblical morality, lifestyle, and worship/prayer to God, then that person's life becomes successful in all seven needs of the human heart. Fulfillment in those seven needs translate to a great life, great marriage, great family, and achievements in the lives who are true disciples of Jesus Christ. Christians should never forget the power of testimony; not just with words but the testimony of a good life. The fruit of godly living is undeniable, and the opportunity this affords the culture changers and reformers is untapped.

Unfortunately, many Christians' lives are not very different from the common culture's narrative, and in this they have no authority to reform. Christians need to escape the social programming and engineering of the common culture and commit to the hard work of spiritual formation and self-government. When we are forged into the spiritual maturity as disciples of Jesus Christ, then the power of the testimony of our lives becomes an irresistible power and the apostolic voice of a new evangelical movement in the West. As Jesus said, *"Wisdom is proved right by her children."*

Chapter 7

Family Heals Everything

The foundation for systemic culture change is marriage and family. Marriage/family is the first cultural and governmental institution that God created. The Genesis narrative and origins of the human race all begin with the establishment of the first family, Adam and Eve. The root of cultural decay and the undoing of cultural stability all hinges on the health and success of marriage and family. Almost every crime and cultural sin is solved by having healthy marriage and family dynamics within that culture. Think about it: There would not be any human trafficking if families were healed and functioning closely to God's design. There are many other examples of areas in our current cultural rot that would be changed by having healthy families but for the sake of expediency, we will not mention them here. What is most important for us to understand is that God was specific in His design when He created the institution of marriage and family. That design is embodied in the theology of the human body which is the gender binary.

Today, the modern Progressive Left understands that it is necessary to break God's gender binary so they can redefine the family. Their goal is to seek levels that would weaken it because they know when families are governed according to God's design, then society cannot be hijacked by humanistic policies and atheistic worldviews. Personal freedom does not include the freedom to misuse, sexually defile or mutilate our bodies with transgender surgeries because freedom can only exist within the bounds of God's permissibility. Freedom requires self-control and self-regulation. The alternative is social and personal anarchy. The proof is found in the statistics on the mental health of sex workers, homosexuals, transgenders, and the divorced. The happiest and healthiest people are those who have healthy marriages and maintain good family relationships. We certainly do not need to be married to be happy, yet generally speaking, happily married people do enjoy the best mental health and the best quality of life.

The Theology of the Human Body

Currently in our culture, there have been profound changes and movements away from the Biblical or Christian worldview, morals, and ethics in every sphere of society from Family, Education, Government, Religion, Media, Economy, and Arts/Entertainment. There is a driver for this type of sea change in our culture. It is the Humanist ethos at work. As we learned earlier,

Humanism believes that the world was constructed from energy and mass which has always existed in some form and has been shaped into its current form by random chance. The natural result of believing that the world was constructed from energy and mass colliding into its current form by chance is that there is no law to govern the morals, ethics, and conduct of people. Humanism sees man as a law unto himself. With this view, humanity can arbitrarily decide what is true and right apart from any other agency. It is a worldview without a governor, except for the heart of man.

The Biblical worldview sees the world as created, ordered, designed, and arranged by the mind, power, and presence of a benevolent Creator God. The Biblical worldview sees purpose in all creation, especially purpose in people because they are made in God's image. In this worldview, humanity is made in the image and likeness of God. Christians see great works of art, creativity, the founding of great cultures, the study of science, biology, engineering and mechanics as an outflow of Imago Dei in humanity. We see intelligent design and order as a witness of God's creative power. The Biblical worldview invites us into the adventure of discovery and gives meaning to life. Humanism can never produce this type of wonder and adventure because there is nothing special about people. Whatever is good, compassionate, and right in society is a hangover from the Christian ethos and Biblical worldview in the West.

In this section, we will focus on the contrast between the Biblical worldview and the humanist worldview as they relate to the human body. Each of these worldviews have implications for the way in which we see the human body and how humanity should live.

God Designed Your Body

The Bible teaches that humanity is the result of a loving God creating them male and female, in His image and likeness. Genesis 1:27 says:

> *"So God created man in his own image, in the image of God he created him; male and female he created them."*

And Psalm 139:13 says:

> *"For you formed my inward parts; you knitted me together in my mother's womb."*

There are many other verses that put forth the idea that humanity has been intimately created and designed by God and humanity has intrinsic value because we reflect Him. This means your own humanity is by design, ordered by God, and created for you to re-image dimensions of His infinite beauty and intelligence. Humanity is not the result of energy and mass randomly arranging itself by chance at some point in the past.

Biologists and other disciplines of life science have discovered amazing truths about the human body. The complexities of the nervous system, reproductive systems, circulatory system, bone structure, and DNA all point to intelligent design. It is a canard to say that the cosmos was the result of pre-existing matter and energy coming together by chance to produce what we see today. When you look at your body, you can see God's creative design, power, order, and most of all His love for you in how He designed you.

Your Body Has Purpose

Those who hold the Judeo-Christian worldview see the expression of God's design in humanity as male and female. Each sex, or gender, equally reflects God's glory in creation, and one is not better than the other. True egalitarianism is a product of the Christian ethos. We can be thankful and proud, whether we are male or female, because both sexes/genders re-image God. Our complex cultural infrastructures run with efficiency because of the male/female binary operating per God's design. Every culture on planet earth is sustained by the male/female binary. The most basic manifestation of this is human reproduction and the most advanced manifestation of the male/female binary is industrialized cultures.

The Christian worldview promotes purpose for each sex/gender in a way that adds intrinsic value that is both absolute and spiritually transcendent beyond the natural world because the male/female reality lives in relationship to a benevolent God. The male/female binary is interdependent on each other for the continuance of life, culture, production, and advancement. The Christian worldview of the male/female binary sees the purpose of the human body in a multiplicity of expressions that are valuable to all. Being a male or female is glorious because our unique sex/gender has identity in God and by God.

God Loves Your Body

Christianity is not uninformed about the presence of evil in the world. Chapter 3 in the book of Genesis reveals the narrative of how death, evil, corruption, and human sin came into existence. God's perfect created world was marred by the Fall of Adam and Eve. Because God created humanity in His image and likeness, He created humanity with the ability to love freely. He honored humanity with the power of free will choice. The ability to love freely and choose self-will came with the responsibility to trust and love God in all things. Authenticity in love only happens when there is a choice to not love. In the temptation, Adam and Eve chose to not trust and love God as they were deceived by Satan.

However, God did not abandon humanity. He promised a Messiah who would reunite God and Man. In that promise, He revealed the story of Messiah through Scripture, and then manifested Messiah in the Man, Jesus Christ. John 3:16 says:

> *"For God so loved the world, that he gave his only Son, that whoever believes in him should not perish but have eternal life."*

God loved your body so much, that He saved it. He also promises to resurrect it into immortality.

There are multiple places in the Bible where we see God healing the body, providing for the body, strengthening the body, and blessing the body. God loves our bodies so much that God the Son died for the redemption of our bodies on a cross. Sin lives in the heart of mankind and expresses itself through the human body. Jesus' sacrifice on the cross for sin is the hope of the salvation for all humanity. Every person knows that they are imperfect and subject to weakness. They make mistakes that cause pain, whether they are Christians or not. Imperfection in people is a witness of an unresolved situation between God and His binary male/female creation. The good news is that God made good on His promise to redeem what was lost in the Fall through Jesus Christ.

Implications of the Theology of the Body ___

The theology of the human body has major implications in all things. Marriage, family, culture, sexuality, ethics, and morals are all shaped by the theology of the body. Because your body is wonderfully and fearfully made in God's image, your body is special. Your body was made for covenant with God because He redeemed it by the blood of His Son, Jesus Christ. The concept of covenant in the ancient world is a binding sacred oath like marriage and beautifully demonstrated in the New Covenant that was cut by the blood of Christ. The human body is just as sacred, as is the soul that lives behind the eyes. The Christian worldview regarding the human body promotes honoring our bodies, loving, caring and protecting our bodies. The leaders who agree with this worldview will always defend the rights of the exploited, the oppressed and the unborn. They work to preserve the innocence of children because it is the logical outflow of believing that people are made in God's image.

Of the two competing worldviews that are struggling for preeminence in our culture, only the Christian worldview produces compassion, order, prosperity, purpose, and protects the inalienable rights of the individual. Humanism is not capable of producing anything but chaos, shifting ethics, amorality, and the devolution of a culture. This is the only logical conclusion of Humanism because human life is not special, and there are no absolutes in the current time/space continuum in which we live. Humanistic truth is found and discovered in the heart of mankind at a particular time of feeling or thinking. Humanism is a progressive philosophy that is bound only by what mankind says is true. It is imperative that Christians begin to see the world through the construct of the Christian worldview and not compromise with humanism and relativism. Understanding the implications of the theology of the human body destroys the LGBTQ+ agenda that has sought to redefine the theology of the human body in terms of humanistic constructs and not Biblical truth. I included this section in this chapter because understanding God's design for human body helps support God's design for marriage and family. Successful marriage and families start with the gender binary of male and female coming together in the sacramental covenant of marriage. As Jesus said, *"Two would become one flesh."* Every time Scripture mentions marriage it is always in the context of God's gender binary: male and female.

Marriage and Family

Since marriage and family is God's design for a cultural foundation, it is important that local churches provide templates, solutions, and examples for young people and older singles to have successful marriages and families. The collective health of any culture is dependent on the success of marriages in that culture, (https://www.psychologytoday.com/us/blog/resolution-not-conflict/201109/happy-marriage-happy-life). For this reason, cultural engineers seek to dismantle the Biblical worldview for the purpose of destroying the family in order to rebuild their vision for a society without God. Humanist social engineers have created two social constructs that have contributed to the decrease of marriage and the decline of intact families These constructs are feminism and no-fault divorce, with the added pressures of the unfair decisions of family courts.

Biblical Feminism — If we look at the Bible in the ways it describes the ideals for marriage and the relational dynamics between men and women, we would see a social ethos of altruism, liberty, honor, and respect between the two genders. The New Testament is emphatic in its description of the types of relational dynamics between men and women that make society function in ways that benefit the whole. The New Testament teaches us that men and women enjoy the same rights as redeemed children of God. We are eternally saved the same; we approach God in prayer the same; we have access to the same gifts of the Holy Spirit; and we hold the same value in the Kingdom of God. The New Testament paints a picture of a radically egalitarian nature between races, nations, and gender. (For a more complete treatment of Biblical Feminism, see my book *Five-Fold Females* also found on Amazon.)

If we were to define Biblical Feminism, we would describe it as follows:

1) Women have the same value as men regarding rights, identity before God, privileges, and the gifts that He bestows on His Beloved Church.

2) Women are to be respected as sisters and loved as wives like Christ loved the Church.

3) Men and women should have the same opportunity and access to education, areas of interest, and professional opportunities.

4) Men and women enjoy a relational dynamic that is altruistic in function. As equals before God, we celebrate the differences in our God-given design, and use our God-given gender to act altruistically to serve the other gender.

This definition of Biblical Feminism is a high view of the New Testament ideal for male and female relational dynamics. Because this definition is an ideal, we all understand that many will fail at living in complete synergy that agrees with it. However, Biblical ideals are the ideals that bend us towards personal and societal behavior, as summed up in Romans 13:10:

"Love does no wrong to a neighbor; therefore, love is the fulfilling of the law."

Seven Spheres Rising: Building Micro-Culture in Babylon

This is verse is the Biblical standard for all human relationships.

Modern humanistic feminism denies the gender difference. Rather than celebrating the altruistic relational dynamics between men and women, modern feminism frames the relational dynamics between men and women as adversarial. Modern feminism teaches that women do not need men. It declares the social construct of patriarchy makes females victims of male oppression. The reality is that there are differences between the genders in terms of strength, biology, physiology, and societal function. These differences can be used positively or negatively. A society governed with an awareness of the Biblical standard of relational dynamics should be the most egalitarian and safe for women. Modern feminism denies the value of masculine energy that a culture needs. It frames marriage and family as oppressive/ repressive institutions. Modern feminism has robbed multitudes of women the joy of marriage and family, leaving many women facing middle-age alone and unhappy. It has also left many men alone and unhappy, too. The social construct of Biblical Feminism, in the opinion of this writer, would bring great benefit to both men and women. The result would be a happy, whole society and culture.

The Damage of No-Fault Divorce — No-Fault divorce is in itself an oxymoron. In a divorce, there is always fault in either one or both parties that contribute to the failure of a marriage. Whether it is adultery, abuse, or disrespect it is the fault of sin in people. What no-fault divorce means is that there need not be any other reason to divorce except for the selfishness in people. It also means that the court will not judge between the parties except in terms of child support and the division of property. If courts actually judged between the offenses of the parties getting divorced, then many would choose not to divorce and work toward healing the offenses that contributed to the breakdown of the relationship instead. Many divorcees regret they divorced their spouse and damaged their family dynamics for the remainder of their lives. There is some divorce that is righteous, as in the case of adultery or abuse, however many divorces are based upon personal decisions of dissatisfaction and selfish motivations. Currently, no-fault divorce has resulted in men paying 50% or more of their wealth in the divorce and losing regular contact with their children over time, with many becoming estranged from them. The societal and cultural cost is staggering in terms of cultural pain and suffering of men, women, and especially the children.

As long as modern feminism and no-fault divorce are promoted by the humanist social engineers, the West will continue to devolve culturally. The good news is that the Church possesses the grace, mandate, and authority from God with His Word to model His design for marriage and family. When Christians begin to think more monolithic regarding God's design for marriage and family, then our opportunity to become a city on a hill for family rapidly increases. Good living is attractive and so are happy families.

Healthy Families Heal Society

The cultural foundation that can bring the fastest reformation to a nation is happy, healthy marriages and families. Good marriages and families promote the best behaviors in humans. They are the prophylaxis to the cultural sickness that defines the current American culture. So much of what ails the West can be directly attributed to the breakdown of the family structure leaving multiple generations of people living in poverty, suffering in prisons, attached to the state through the welfare system, and living in depressive cycles that last a lifetime – oftentimes becoming a generational cyle on the family line. Family heals everything. Healing the American family is absolutely necessary for healing the common culture. Only the Biblical worldview and the promotion of the Christian faith in the West will reform it in ways that produce the most prosperity and happiness for the people.

Concluding Encouragments

The main thrust of this work is not to provide an in-depth treatment on the subject of sociology and cultural reformation, but to cast a long, high vision for the future of America and the West. Reading this book might possibly discourage the reader but the truth of the matter is that with God there is always hope. The West is at a crossroads between two worldviews. One worldview leads to a cultural renaissance; the other worldview speeds the decline of the nation. It remains to be seen if America devolves slowly in a way similar to the Roman Empire, or if it will be reborn by Spirit-filled Christians who become active in the real work of saving a nation. Although those who commit to fight the great spiritual battle for the future of America are indeed committing to a multi-generational work, we should be encouraged to stay the course and celebrate our incremental progress and achievements.

Cultural reformation is a slow and patient work that with time will be remembered in the eternal Courts of Heaven as each one of us receives our crown of glory for work done in His Name. You, dear reader, should be both alarmed and encouraged. Alarmed because an anesthetized Church has been slow walking the nation to its death; encouraged because building micro-cultures always results in a cultural shift in the long run.

Benjamin Franklin said it best:

"Only a virtuous people are capable of freedom. As nations become corrupt and vicious, they have more need of masters."

This is the true and current set of circumstances in America. It is time for the Church to become virtuous, brave and active in building micro-cultures that become culture.

Solus virtuosus et fortis Christianus gloriam sapit!

About the Author

D r. Rob Covell is the Provost at Wagner University, Pasadena CA. He is author of the popular *Five-Fold Females, Virum: How to Become a High-Value Man, The Revelation of Hope: A Commentary on the Book of Revelation, Dawrash: How To Read Your Bible and Understand It, Diakrino: How is God Judging the World Today?* and many others. Dr. Rob is also a church consultant, educational reformer, and lover of Jesus Christ. Dr. Rob is committed to societal transformation through Christian education and works to return America back to her Christian ethos that made her the greatest nation. Dr. Rob is happily married to his wife, Carolyn. They have four adult children and one amazing grandson, "Little Rex."

MORE BOOKS BY DR. ROB COVELL AVAILABLE ON AMAZON!

VIRUM: How to Become A High-Value Man

Written to a generation of young men on their quest to become great, VIRUM is for those who are seeking principles of living that will empower them to succeed in every metric of life. If you're looking for fatherly wisdom and a direct approach on how to manage your life, VIRUM is a must read for any man who is serious about self-improvement, personal growth, and prosperity of soul!

READY FOR PURCHASE ON AMAZON NOW!

FIVE-FOLD FEMALES

This best seller, *Five-Fold Females,* will invite you into the journey of reclaiming the passionate Christ-centered egalitarianism of the Early Church. If you are a woman in ministry, this book will help you effectively position yourself in the Body of Christ for your divine mission and purpose.

GET YOURS ON AMAZON!

www.ingramcontent.com/pod-product-compliance
Lightning Source LLC
Chambersburg PA
CBHW050922260726
48660CB00001B/341